Praise for *The ABCs of Educational Testing: Demystifying the Tools That Shape Our Schools*

"W. James Popham has done it again! He has found the topic that educators must understand in this quantitative age—testing and accountability—and once more writes with clarity, grace, and a little levity about technical matters. I can't think of a better way to communicate the essential information that on its face may look daunting. His book is approachable and helpful."

—Eva Baker
Founding Director, CRESST
Distinguished Research Professor, UCLA

"This is a wonderfully entertaining book about a most serious matter—what teachers and other educators need to know about testing—written by one of our nation's finest educators and most engaging writers. The ABCs of Educational Testing is a highly readable, engaging, and authoritative book that allows teachers to design, use, and interpret educational tests in an appropriate way.

It ensures that educational tests will reflect the purpose they were intended to fulfill, making the data obtained useful to educators instead of alien to them. It provides the basics of test design and interpretation in a lucid and engaging manner and is highly recommended for educators, particularly teachers and school board members. It provides them with everything they need to know about test construction and interpretation—and it does so in a lively manner.

The ABCs of Educational Testing will help correct the inappropriate and misleading use of educational testing, one of our nation's growth industries."

—David C. Berliner
Regents' Professor Emeritus
Mary Lou Fulton Teachers College, Arizona State University

"In the wonderful The ABCs of Educational Testing, *W. James Popham says, 'Too few folks who should know something about educational testing do not,' and sadly, he is right. If people in his five target audiences (teachers, educational administrators, educational policymakers, parents of school-age children, and everyday citizens) read this entertaining (yes, 'entertaining,' a word not often associated with educational testing!) and informative book it would go a long way toward correcting this unfortunate reality.*

With his unique phrases and word choices (e.g., 'I find myself magnetically drawn to a textbook that I wrote myself.') W. James Popham clearly describes and explains the critical aspects of educational testing that need widespread understanding. He stresses the importance of tests being used and interpreted for the purpose for which they are intended, and shows why many of the tests used to evaluate schools, teachers and students are inappropriate. He does this through 10 short chapters that illuminate his 9 assessment-related understandings and his concerns about the lack of assessment literacy. In particular, he provides clarity to often confusing concepts such as validity and reliability and fairness in testing.

Popham says that 'hands down' the chapter on validity is the most important, but for me the most important chapter is the one on formative assessment, which he identifies as 'inexcusably underused.' I consider this to be the most important because my major involvement is with K-12 teachers and administrators and until recently most teachers and administrators, through no fault of their own, have not understood the instructional uses of assessment. This is changing because of the influence of people like W. James Popham, Rick Stiggins and Dylan Wiliam. Popham provides a definition of formative assessment that stresses that it is a process (not an event) that provides evidence, which enables teachers to adjust their teaching and students to adjust their learning strategies so that greater learning takes place. Traditionally teachers have put a number on everything students do and every number has been part of student grades regardless of the purpose of the assessment, but the research shows that it is descriptive feedback and identifying student understandings and misconceptions while the learning is going on that makes the greatest contribution to improving student achievement. W. James Popham understands this and makes the case that it is 'remarkably effective' and 'seriously underutilized.'

To sum up, this book is a must read for the five audiences that Popham identifies because it is critical that everyone has the 9 assessment related understandings that he so eloquently and clearly explains and describes."

—Ken O'Connor
Consultant/Author/Former High School Teacher and
Curriculum Coordinator
Assess for Consulting Inc.

"With The ABC's of Educational Testing, W. James Popham continues his quest to support and enlighten all who have a stake in improving our educational systems. This short but immensely powerful instrument is in the form of a 10-chapter "chat" about the often-inscrutable business of student testing in our schools.

Popham's book explains the sometimes impenetrable language of educational testing in a way that is easy to comprehend and appreciate. Each chapter illuminates a specific issue that that affords the reader a clear translation of the understanding, meaning, and important role of that particular issue in student assessment.

The book is precisely directed at five audiences who would have a clear impact on testing in schools: classroom teachers, educational administrators, educational policymakers, parents of school-aged children, and everyday citizens. It has the lofty yet simple aim of assuring that educational testing is understood and used as a potent tool for student learning rather than in other more pejorative and inappropriate ways.

Popham's inimitable style is sure to capture the interest and engagement of any reader with an interest in student assessment. This book will be an indispensable guide for individuals and groups who want to help understand, monitor, and provide guidance for educational testing in their schools."

—Frank Philip, Ph.D.
Arts Education Assessment Consultant
Independent Student Assessment Consultant;
Former Director
National Conference on Student Assessment, CCSSO

The ABCs of Educational Testing

Demystifying the Tools That Shape Our Schools

W. James Popham

CORWIN

A SAGE Publishing Company

FOR INFORMATION:

Corwin
A SAGE Company
2455 Teller Road
Thousand Oaks, California 91320
www.corwin.com

SAGE Publications Ltd.
1 Oliver's Yard
55 City Road
London EC1Y 1SP
United Kingdom

SAGE Publications India Pvt. Ltd.
B 1/I 1 Mohan Cooperative Industrial Area
Mathura Road, New Delhi 110 044
India

SAGE Publications Asia-Pacific Pte. Ltd.
3 Church Street
#10–04 Samsung Hub
Singapore 049483

Acquisitions Editor: Jessica Allan
Associate Editor: Kimberly Greenberg
Editorial Assistant: Katie Crilley
Production Editor: Veronica Stapleton Hooper
Copy Editor: Janet Ford
Typesetter: C&M Digitals (P) Ltd.
Proofreader: Barbara Coster
Indexer: Michael Ferreira
Cover Designer: Anupama Krishnan
Marketing Manager: Lisa Lysne

Library of Congress Cataloging-in-Publication Data

Names: Popham, W. James, author.

Title: The ABCs of educational testing : demystifying the tools that shape our schools / W. James Popham.

Description: Thousand Oaks, California : Corwin, 2016. | Includes bibliographical references and index.

Identifiers: LCCN 2016030835 | ISBN 9781506351513 (pbk. : alk. paper)

Subjects: LCSH: Educational tests and measurements—United States.

Classification: LCC LB3051 .P61415 2016 | DDC 371.26—dc23
LC record available at https://lccn.loc.gov/2016030835

This book is printed on acid-free paper.

16 17 18 19 20 10 9 8 7 6 5 4 3 2 1

Contents

 A supplement to *The ABCs of Educational Testing* is available at
http://resources.corwin.com/PophamABCsTesting.

Preface

Educational testing has not been a lifelong interest of mine. Indeed, not until midcareer did I devote any serious thinking to the care and feeding of educational tests. Let me explain. Near the close of my college days as a philosophy major, I discovered that the workplace was not eager to hire novice Aristotelian philosophers. Accordingly, with no job prospects before me, I decided to stay in college for an extra year, earn a teaching credential, and then try to land a job as a high school teacher. I should confess, at that time, I found small children to be thoroughly repellant. Consequently, becoming an elementary teacher was definitely not in the cards. Nonetheless, the idea of teaching adolescents seemed potentially endurable.

Soon, I found myself enrolled in a seriously shabby teacher-education program—a program that taught me next to nothing about how to teach. As that teacher-education travesty was nearing its conclusion, I found myself assigned to serve as a student teacher under the guidance of a marvelous supervising teacher. Out there in the real world, she tossed me enough instructional rope so that I made it through my student-teaching assignment. Then, after a couple of happy years teaching high school in eastern Oregon, I enrolled in a doctoral program at Indiana University where I majored in instructional procedures—a program designed to make me a teacher educator who could supply prospective teachers with accurate insights about instruction.

And that's where the first half of my career was centered, as a teacher educator in the UCLA Graduate School of Education providing instructional strategies and tactics to would-be teachers. Moreover, I really enjoyed trying to train prospective teachers—sometimes almost a thousand per year—hoping to supply them with the tools they'd need to become instructional superstars.

But in the late 1970s, many of my former UCLA students—the ones who had been teaching for a while—began telling me that although they were trying to implement the instructional techniques I'd been touting, their instruction was becoming more heavily influenced by the need to have their students succeed on upcoming, important educational tests. After a number of such conversations with my former students, I became convinced that if genuinely significant consequences were going to be based on students' test scores, then whatever was measured by those tests would surely be stressed instructionally. Whether a test's results were being used to evaluate a state's schools or to determine the awarding of a student's high school diploma, the significance of high-import tests had transformed those educational tests into powerful curricular magnets.

With this recognition regarding the curricular impact of educational tests, and a realization that most of the tests being used in our schools had not been fashioned by individuals who knew all that much about instruction, I consciously decided to make a shift in my career path, turning from an emphasis on instruction toward a focus on educational measurement. Much measurement-related reading and studying followed, for I really needed to learn about educational testing pretty much from scratch. For the last three decades, then, I've attempted to center most of my thinking, speaking, and writing on educational testing—what it is, how it is used, and how it can be improved.

Educational Tests: Potent Tools

After just a few years pursuing this new focus, I arrived at a significant conclusion that I still believe to be true. In a nutshell, it is that educational testing constitutes the most cost-effective way to improve our schools. From an *instructional* perspective, a well-formed educational test can provide teachers with needed clarity regarding the specific skills and knowledge they wish to promote for the students in their classrooms. Test-clarified curricular targets can help teachers devise more accurately targeted instructional activities. Turning from instruction to *evaluation,* the use of appropriate educational tests can contribute to sound decisions regarding how successful a teacher's instruction activities actually were. That is, which instructional segments worked well, which instructional segments were so-so, and which instructional segments simply flopped?

> Educational testing constitutes the most cost-effective way to improve our schools.

When there are *any* significant consequences associated with a test's usage, then what's tested will almost certainly be taught. And because the dominant factor we employ to evaluate instruction has sensibly been students' learning, then the tests we employ must be suitable for that mission. Tawdry tests, when used for instruction or evaluation, can have seriously harmful effects on the way our children are educated. Terrific tests, however, can have a decisively positive impact on teaching and learning. And if you consider the often nontrivial costs associated with many improvement-focused educational strategies—such as reducing class sizes—then the cost-effectiveness of excellent educational testing becomes apparent.

UNDERSTANDING EDUCATIONAL TESTING'S BASICS

If well-formed educational tests can have a beneficial impact on the way we educate our children, then more people need to know how to distinguish between educational tests that are wonderful from those that are woeful. But, currently, most of us are busy. Consequently, a common response from educators—and even from parents who have children in school—is to "leave educational testing to the specialists." After all, busy educators and busy parents reasonably assume that the tests being used in our schools are appropriate. What I've learned during the past thirty years, however, is that many of the tests currently used in this nation are flat-out wrong for their intended measurement missions.

Accordingly, I wrote this book with the explicit intention of translating seemingly off-putting technical notions into more accessible language. In this book you will encounter nine key assessment-related understandings. You'll find one of these understandings presented in every chapter's wrap-up section called *Takeaway Time*. Each understanding encapsulates the most important thing I hope you'll take away from that particular chapter. If you spend time to master those nine understandings, then *you* can be in a position to have an influence on the educational tests of concern to you. In the book's final chapter you'll be presented with a set of potential action options that you might wish to undertake as a consequence of your increased understandings regarding educational testing. The book can be read solo or it can form the grist for a study group during which the content of the book's chapters—at a group-determined pace—can be considered.

In an attempt to support readers as they wrestle with this book, after I had written it, I bopped out an *Online Supplement* containing a set of additional activities for each of its ten chapters. Most helpful, I suspect, for groups engaged in a collaborative study of the book's issues, the materials in the supplement can also be used by solo readers. In addition, there are separate Prefaces to the *Online Supplement* for each of the book's five audiences. The *Online Supplement* can be obtained gratis via the publisher's website (http://resources.corwin.com/PophamABCsTesting).

I am not suggesting that every reader of this rather short book should then be regarded as a measurement specialist. However, if you have grasped the book's nine understandings, or almost all of them, then you will be in a position to enlist the services of a measurement specialist who can be tasked with supplying a *plain-language* report to those concerned.

As you wander your way through the book's ten tantalizing chapters, you'll sometimes encounter technical terms. Because, as you'll see in the book, a few of those terms are employed in what might seem to be a counterintuitive fashion by the measurement community. Accordingly, I have provided a glossary at the close of this book, which contains brief definitions of the book's terms identified in an *italicized and boldface* font. Educational testing is laden with no more jargon than any other specialization, and you'll quickly see that most of the terms that you encounter in the glossary actually describe very commonsense concepts or procedures. In the days ahead, if you know you're going to take part in any kind of "real world" formal or informal discussion regarding educational testing, a rapid review of the glossary's definitions might come in handy. No one, after all, wants to be regarded as having tumbled from testing's turnip truck.

There's also an index at the close of the book, but its story line is even less entrancing than what's found in the glossary. Nor, indeed, will you be able to rely on the book's index as a teaching tool—unless you happen to be working with someone who is alphabetically challenged.

I hope this preface makes clear how critical educational testing is in the education of children. If the book itself helps you grasp testing's importance, perhaps what you've learned will incline you to help improve whatever educational testing is going on around you. Improved educational testing unarguably translates into improved education for our students.

W.J.P.

About the Author

W. James Popham has spent the bulk of his educational career as a teacher. His first teaching assignment, for example, was in a small eastern Oregon high school where he taught English and social studies while serving as yearbook advisor, class sponsor, and unpaid tennis coach. That recompense meshed ideally with the quality of his coaching.

Most of Dr. Popham's teaching career was at UCLA, where for nearly thirty years he taught courses in instructional methods for prospective teachers as well as courses in evaluation and measurement for graduate students. At UCLA, he won several distinguished teaching awards. In January 2000, he was recognized by *UCLA Today* as one of UCLA's top twenty professors of the 20th century. (He notes that the 20th century was a full-length century, unlike the current abbreviated one.) In 1992, he took early retirement from UCLA after learning that emeritus professors received free parking.

Because at UCLA he was acutely aware of the perishability of professors who failed to publish, he spent his non-teaching hours affixing words to paper. The result is more than two hundred journal articles and more than thirty books. Many of these books have been translated into Spanish, Portuguese, Arabic, French, Farsi, Chinese, Japanese, Korean, and Canadian.

His most recent books are *Classroom Assessment: What Teachers Need to Know,* 8th edition (2017), *Mastering Assessment* (2011), and *Assessment for Educational Leaders* (2006), Pearson; *Evaluating America's Teachers: Mission Possible?* (2013), *Everything School Leaders Need to Know About Assessment* (2010), and *The ABCs of Educational Testing: Demystifying the Tools That Shape Our Schools* (2017), Corwin; *The Truth About Testing* (2001), *Test Better, Teach Better* (2003), *Transformative Assessment* (2008), *Instruction That Measures Up* (2009), and *Transformative Assessment in Action* (2011), ASCD; *America's "Failing" Schools* (2005), Routledge; *Unlearned Lessons* (2009), Harvard Education Press. He encourages purchase of these books because he regards their semi-annual royalties as psychologically reassuring.

In 1978, Dr. Popham was elected to the presidency of the American Educational Research Association (AERA). He was also the founding editor of *Educational Evaluation and Policy Analysis,* a quarterly journal published by AERA. A Fellow of the Association, he has attended each year's AERA meeting since his first in 1958. He is inordinately compulsive.

In 1968, Dr. Popham established IOX Assessment Associates, an R&D group that formerly created statewide student achievement tests for a dozen states. He has personally passed all of those tests, largely because of his unlimited access to the tests' answer keys.

In 2002, the National Council on Measurement in Education presented him with its Award for Career Contributions to Educational Measurement. In 2009, he was appointed to the National Assessment Governing Board by Secretary of Education, Arne Duncan. In 2014, he received an honorary doctorate of public service from his alma mater, the University of Portland in Oregon. Dr. Popham's complete 45-page, single-spaced vita can be requested. It is really dull reading.

1

Why Fuss With Educational Testing?

This is a book about the basics of educational testing. But you might reasonably ask, why on earth would anyone actually wish to learn about the basics of educational testing? Answering this question is the focus of the book's first chapter. In this chapter I hope to convince you that many people, including *you*, really do need to understand the basics of educational testing.

But first, ever so briefly, let's look at what these "basics" of educational testing are. The title of this book, *The ABCs of Educational Testing,* was chosen because most people believe that the alphabet includes the fundamental building blocks of learning. Once children have mastered their ABCs, they're usually then capable of learning just about anything. What you'll learn in the ensuing pages is a handful of foundational concepts and procedures linked to the testing that routinely goes on in our schools.

Specialists in almost any field often assign distinctive labels to their field's concepts and procedures. Typically, those labels are regarded as necessary because the concepts and procedures involved are being used by specialists in subtly *atypical* ways. Good intentions notwithstanding, the result of such distinctive labeling is that a specialization's content frequently ends up becoming essentially incomprehensible and even mysterious or off-putting to nonspecialists. The field of educational testing is no exception. I am not suggesting any willful camouflaging on the part of testing experts, only the understandable tendency of specialists to employ terminology that best reflects the nuances of their field.

Happily, the actual ABCs of educational testing, contrary to today's widely held view, are understandable *to anyone.* Moreover, there really aren't all that many educational-testing basics. Yes, the true ABCs of educational testing are relatively few in number and, even more importantly, can be readily comprehended by just about everyone. Accordingly, don't anticipate being baffled by the complexity of what you'll encounter in the following pages. The central concepts and procedures of educational testing are neither complicated nor excessively mathematical.

WHO IS THIS BOOK'S TARGET AUDIENCE?

By now you realize that a reader of this book is going to learn some basic stuff about educational testing, and learn it so well that—if asked—this reader can accurately explain this stuff to others. For whom, then, was this book actually written?

Five Target Audiences for a "Basics of Educational Testing" Book

- **Classroom Teachers.** Teachers need to understand how the quality of classroom tests can enhance—or can inhibit—their students' learning. Teachers also need to know how to discern whether the external tests they are required to use are in fact suitable for those tests' alleged functions.

- **Educational Administrators.** If educational administrators understand the contributions and limitations of educational tests, those administrators can better guide teachers regarding the appropriate uses not only of teacher-made tests but also about the appropriate roles for externally imposed exams.
- **Educational Policymakers.** If school board members and elected legislators understand whether particular tests yield evidence that's supportive of evaluative judgments about schooling, those policymakers can make more defensible decisions about the education provided in schools for which such policymakers are responsible.
- **Parents of School-Age Children.** Parents of children who are currently in school, or parents of younger children who will soon be in school, increasingly recognize that children's scores on educational tests can have a huge and sometimes lasting impact on decisions affecting children's in-school and beyond-school lives. Accordingly, parents may wish to know whether the educational tests used with their children are actually appropriate for making those decisions.
- **Everyday Citizens.** Because a society entrusts those who operate its schools with the responsibility to transmit and improve that society's culture, and because educational tests continue to play an important role in the way our schools operate, all citizens have both a right and a responsibility to see whether their tax-supported schools are performing successfully. To do so, citizens need to know if the evidence of school success based on students' test scores is accurate.

I tried to write *The ABCs of Educational Testing* for all five of these audiences. That's right, the book was written for classroom teachers, educational administrators, educational policymakers, parents of school-age children, and everyday citizens. How on earth did I acquire the audacity to tackle all five audiences simultaneously—in one single swipe? Let me tell you.

A few paragraphs ago, I argued that the most essential understandings regarding educational testing are relatively simple and, beyond that, are readily comprehensible to *anyone*. Well, I haven't altered that opinion already—after all, it was only a few paragraphs ago. I continue to believe that the ABCs of educational testing are understandable. What this belief translates into, therefore, is the conviction that if I can do a solid job in explaining what's meant by the key concepts and procedures of educational testing, those explanations can be grasped by members of any of the five potential target audiences identified above.

WHY THESE UNDERSTANDINGS?

If you look back for a moment at the five potential audiences for this book, odds are that you'll discover you fall in one or more of the five groups identified. You might be a parent of a fourth grader, a high-school English teacher, a member of a district school board, a city council member, or simply a citizen who cares about the well-being of our nation's schools. If you happen to fall outside those five groups, however, you might try pretending you're an educator or a parent as you complete the book. Extra motivation, even if mildly contrived, can often contribute to one's understanding.

A reasonable question you might ask yourself is, "So what?" Or, using other words, "Supposing that I do grasp the testing-related understandings about to be dished up in this book, what on earth would I ever be able to do with such understandings?" It is a reasonable question.

Well, the final chapter of this book will lay out a menu of potential actions that different readers of the book could take, and you'll definitely want to review those suggestions. However, even at this early point in the book, here are a few brief examples of possible action options available to members of each of the book's five target audiences.

Classroom teachers will be better able to generate their own tests to be used for particular purposes, such as improving ongoing instruction or evaluating the success of an entire semester's worth of instruction.

Educational administrators, such as school principals or assistant principals, can not only more skillfully support teachers' creation of effective classroom assessments, but school-site administrators can better discern which types of standardized tests are appropriate—or inappropriate—for evaluating a school's success.

Educational policymakers, for instance, an elected member of a suburban school board, after determining the degree to which students' performances on particular standardized achievement tests are truly indicative of how well the district's students are taught, can demand the use of tests that accurately evaluate instructional quality.

Parents of school-age children can first determine whether their children's teachers appear to use classroom tests in a way that's apt to enhance students' learning, and then—if necessary—support a teacher's greater use of classroom assessments designed to support instruction.

Everyday citizens can determine if media reports regarding students' performances on standardized tests are truly indicative of the degree to which those students were successfully taught and, if necessary, lobby for the use of more evaluatively accurate standardized tests.

In sum, the basic understandings promoted in this book are not merely "nice to know" for their own sake, but beyond that can serve as the springboards for readers to undertake a make-a-difference action. As indicated above, in Chapter 10 a batch of potential action options will be presented for the reader who—by that time—is most likely a *test-knowledgeable* reader.

CONVERSATIONS IN THE OFFING

It is often helpful to readers, particularly to readers of a possibly too technical book, if they know what's coming. Because the book deals with potentially complicated test-related topics, my treatment of those topics might easily become too technical for widespread understanding. Therefore, I have kept the book's language sublimely informal—much as if I were having a casual conversation with an educator in a school's Teachers' Lounge, or chatting with a passenger sitting next to me on an airplane. During such conversations, because I am supposed to know more about the book's content than most readers, I'll typically be the *explainer* while the reader is, I suppose, the *explained-to*.

To help you to get an early-on fix regarding your current capacity to understand many of the concepts and procedures treated in the following pages, you'll see on page 8 *A Confidence Inventory About Educational Assessment.* Please take a few moments to complete the inventory by anonymously registering the degree of confidence you *currently* possess if you were asked to undertake each of the ten activities described in this self-report inventory.

To avoid a potential terminology mix-up, however, before you tangle with the inventory, please recognize that in most of today's written materials about educational testing, the following labels are regarded as essentially interchangeable:

*Educational Testing = Educational
Assessment = Educational Measurement*

Almost everyone understands what is meant by "an educational test." Yet, such tests (also called examinations or exams) are sometimes thought to consist only of the sorts of exams that most of today's adults experienced when they themselves were students in school—for example, tests incorporating multiple-choice, short answer, and essay items. To counteract such thinking, when referring to a "test," many writers prefer to employ the descriptive labels of "assessment" or "measurement," which often bring to mind a wider variety of useful educational testing techniques, such as performance exams, oral quizzes, or collaborative problem-solving tasks. Although, at least for the present, the label educational "assessment" seems to be the most fashionable descriptor for educational testing, from this point on in the book, please regard the labels "testing," "assessment," and "measurement" as equivalent descriptors.

Now, with this terminology clarification in mind, please complete the self-report confidence inventory you'll find on page 8. On page 9 following the inventory, you will find a brief scoring guide for the confidence inventory. After finishing the inventory, please give the scoring guide a brief look. When you have almost completed your reading of this book, you will again be provided with a copy of the confidence inventory so that you can once again complete the inventory to see if there have been any meaningful differences in your confidence level regarding certain aspects of educational assessment.

EDUCATIONAL ASSESSMENT

A Confidence Inventory About Educational Assessment

VC = Very Confident	FC = Fairly Confident	LC = A Little Confident	NC = Not Confident at All

Directions: This inventory is intended to determine how confident you are with key educational assessment content. *Anonymously,* please indicate your level of confidence if *you* were asked to carry out each of the ten activities described in the inventory. Circle one of the following responses for each activity.

Suppose *you* were asked to	How confident would *you* be?			
1. describe to a family member what is meant by the label "student affect."	VC	FC	LC	NC
2. explain to a friend what the three chief purposes of educational testing are.	VC	FC	LC	NC
3. help settle an argument between two teachers by clarifying the difference between "validity" and "reliability."	VC	FC	LC	NC
4. make a brief oral presentation during a meeting of parents describing the key concepts of formative assessment.	VC	FC	LC	NC
5. describe to a parent how teachers should evaluate classroom tests intended to support teaching.	VC	FC	LC	NC
6. write a short note to a friend who is a state legislator in another state describing what is meant by "instructional sensitivity."	VC	FC	LC	NC
7. explain to a school's principal why there are different kinds of reliability evidence.	VC	FC	LC	NC
8. describe to a new acquaintance how today's concept of assessment validity differs from yesteryear's notion of assessment validity.	VC	FC	LC	NC
9. identify for a group of everyday citizens why it is the responsibility of those who design score reports to make them readily understandable.	VC	FC	LC	NC
10. explain to a newly elected member of a local school board how today's educational tests should incorporate assessment fairness.	VC	FC	LC	NC

A Half-Century March Toward High-Stakes Testing

Educational testing has not always been such a big deal. Years ago, when I was a high-school teacher in Oregon, my students were obliged to complete a pair of nationally *standardized tests* every year. (Note: The glossary at the end of this book contains brief definitions of the book's terms identified in an *italicized and boldface* font.) Back then, however, annual standardized test-taking was mostly a ritual rather than an influencer of what went on in my school.

But this indifference to standardized testing evaporated in 1965 with the passage of the Elementary and Secondary Education Act (ESEA), a federal law of enormous significance. Whereas, prior to ESEA, almost all monies for public schools had come from state and local taxes, this groundbreaking 1965 statute supplied really serious federal dollars to state and local school systems. Although the vast majority of the funds needed to operate U.S. public schools were, despite the enactment of ESEA, still provided by state and local tax dollars, ESEA's new fiscal contributions to public schooling were greeted with elation by most state and local education officials.

CONFIDENCE INVENTORY INTERPRETATION GUIDE

This self-report confidence inventory is intended to help determine your perceived confidence in understanding a set of assessment-related concepts and procedures by securing your estimated confidence in explaining such content to others. To determine your total score on the inventory, simply assign the following per-item scores: VC = 3 points, FC = 2 points, SC = 1 point, and NC (or no response) = 0 points. Overall, then, the confidence you possess prior to reading this book can range from a high of 30 points to a low of zero. You may find it illuminating to recomplete the confidence inventory after reading the book. If you wish to retake the inventory, it is presented again on page 125.

Almost overnight, based exclusively on the evaluative requirements of 1965's ESEA, make-a-difference *educational evaluation* was born in the United States.

But there was a catch. Given the unprecedented nature of the federal funds provided via ESEA, many federal lawmakers were concerned that those funds might not be wisely spent by state-level and local education officials. Led by Robert F. Kennedy, at that time the junior U.S. senator from New York, key requirements were inserted into the final version of the legislation so that state recipients of federal ESEA dollars were obliged to evaluate "this year's" ESEA-supported educational programs in order to be eligible for "next year's" federal largesse. Almost overnight, based exclusively on the evaluative requirements of 1965's ESEA, make-a-difference *educational evaluation* was born in the United States.

Because it was generally conceded that the effectiveness of ESEA-supported educational programs should be evaluated chiefly according to how much students had learned, almost all early evaluations called for students' scores on standardized tests to serve as the most important evaluative evidence. Because such nationally standardized tests as the *Iowa Tests of Basic Skills* or the *Stanford Achievement Tests* were usually sitting on the shelves in many district offices, and were widely thought to be credible measures of students' learning, those tests soon became anointed as the chief tools for evaluating educational quality in our schools.

Relentlessly, an ESEA-fueled view of educational evaluation was accepted by more and more Americans—educators and noneducators alike—that students' scores on standardized tests provided the best evidence regarding how well a group of students had been taught. Even today, it is a view widely held. As you will see in Chapter 4, however, it is a view that is often wrong—and harmfully wrong at that!

Because schools whose students performed below expectations on a state's annual standardized test could receive serious federal sanctions, the function of such tests was to make educators responsible for the quality of their instructional endeavors. As a result of this usage, these exams soon became known as *accountability tests*. For the most part, such annually administered accountability tests were either an off-the-shelf commercially produced standardized achievement test or, in some instances, a state-developed standardized test designed to measure students' mastery of a state's officially designated knowledge and skills. Students' performances on accountability tests, therefore, soon became the front-and-center freeway for evaluating the nation's schools.

In addition to standardized tests' evaluative function based on the performances of student *groups,* such tests also began being used to make important decisions about *individual students.* Given an increasing belief on the part of many U.S. citizens during the 1960s that some students—without being able to read, write, and compute—were still receiving high-school diplomas, widespread calls were heard for educators to measure students' minimum competencies. Indeed, students' passing a minimum-competency test soon became a high-school diploma hurdle in about half of our states. Students who failed to demonstrate, via their performances on such "minimum competency tests," that they possessed at least rudimentary skills in reading, mathematics, and writing—after having been given several opportunities to retake a failed exam—were not granted a high-school diploma.

When we couple the negative consequences of a school's students' failing to score well on an annual ESEA-required accountability test with the diploma-denial function of high-school graduation tests in many of our states, it is understandable that these standardized tests were soon referred to as *high-stakes tests.* Unquestionably, they were.

But, laws can be revised, and during the more than fifty years that ESEA has exerted its powerful influence on American schooling, this federal law has been congressionally reauthorized a number of times. And, not surprisingly, in each of those revisions, changes—sometimes substantial—were made. For instance, an influential reauthorization of ESEA in 2002 was the *No Child Left Behind Act* (NCLB), which carried with it a new series of daunting penalties for educators whose students failed to perform satisfactorily on annual state dispensed, but federally overseen, accountability tests. The most recent reauthorization of ESEA was a December 2015 bipartisan enactment of the *Every Student Succeeds Act* (ESSA). ESSA continued the NCLB requirement for annual testing of students at many grade levels, but assigned a substantial degree of oversight for implementing those assessment requirements to the states rather than to the federal government.

The *National Assessment of Educational Progress* (NAEP) is a congressionally authorized project of the U.S. Department of Education periodically assessing, on a sampling basis throughout the United States, students' performance in key subject areas. Because earlier administrations of NAEP revealed that different states had set markedly different levels of performance for students to be classified as satisfactory, in 2010 the federal government subsidized two state-level assessment consortia. Their mission was to create annually administered tests suitable for determining students' status with respect to the Common Core State Standards (CCSS), a set of curricular aims developed by two nongovernmental organizations intended for adoption by many, if not all, states.

Those assessment consortia, the Partnership for the Assessment of Readiness for College and Careers (PARCC) and the Smarter Balanced Assessment Consortia (SBAC), developed the necessary accountability tests suitable for measuring students' status with respect to the CCSS, but considerable backlash developed in various quarters of the nation against what some perceived to be a "federally imposed" national curriculum.

Because of political and parent opposition and other considerations, a number of states exited from their original membership in one of the two assessment consortia, preferring instead to develop—usually with external contractors' assistance—their own accountability tests. Membership in one of the consortia (PARCC) has dropped precipitously low—including, at this writing, only a handful of states—while the other consortium (SBAC) has fifteen state members.

Given the uncertainty regarding how state education leaders will choose to implement ESSA in their own states, it is difficult to foretell how states' accountability tests will be established, and equally unclear about the assessment-related role to be played by the curricular aims embodied in the CCSS. Some states have simply adopted the CCSS as is, but used a different descriptor to label those goals. Other states have engaged in a substantial effort to identify suitable curricular targets and ways of assessing students' achievement of those targets.

THE FORMATIVE-ASSESSMENT PROCESS: INEXCUSABLY UNDERUSED

About twenty years ago a pair of British researchers, Paul Black and Dylan Wiliam, published a comprehensive review of roughly 250 sound research studies dealing with the *instructional* dividends of classroom assessment. Based on a meticulous review of studies involving teachers who employed classroom tests to improve students' learning, Black and Wiliam centered their attention on the use of classroom assessments to help teachers decide whether to make any adjustments in their ongoing instruction, or to help students decide whether they needed to make adjustments in the ways they were trying to learn things. This use of classroom assessment as an *instructional* illuminator is referred to as *formative assessment.* Black and Wiliam concluded "conclusively that formative assessment does improve learning" (Black & Wiliam, 1998, p. 61).

> Students whose teachers employ the formative-assessment process almost always learn far more than do students in classes taught by teachers who fail to employ formative assessment.

The gains in student learning attributed to teachers' using the formative-assessment process are not only consistent, they are substantial. Students whose teachers employ the formative-assessment process almost always learn far more than do students in classes taught by teachers who fail to employ formative assessment. As a consequence of the persistent and powerful payoffs of classroom formative assessment, it is apparent that the formative-assessment process should be more widely employed in our nation's classrooms. Yet, even though more pervasive use of formative assessment should clearly be encouraged, at the moment far too few of our nation's students are experiencing it. In Chapter 8 of this book, you'll see how formative assessment works.

TAKEAWAY TIME

Here's the most important understanding I hope you acquire as you read this chapter, complete with a handy label to help you remember it.

> Twin Motivations for Assessment Knowledge: *Those who care about our schools should understand educational-assessment basics, not only because inappropriate tests often lead to mistaken high-stakes decisions but also because classroom formative assessment is being underused.*

Let's say that, while reading the chapter—often nodding emphatically in agreement as you did so—you internalized the above understanding. You can surely agree that there is nothing that's technically off-putting about this understanding. A straightforward translation might be that many folks need to understand educational testing because (1) we're frequently using the wrong tests to make key decisions and (2) we're not using formative assessment as much as we should. That two-part idea, or some paraphrased rendition of it, is what you should have gained from this opening chapter.

2

Three Primary Purposes of Educational Testing[1]

M any of our students are not being educated as well these days as they should be. A key cause for this calamity is that we often use the wrong tests to make our most important educational decisions. What's so sad about this state of affairs is that few people—including many educators—actually understand how it is that today's off-target educational tests are contributing to diminished educational quality (Popham, 2017).

When future educational historians look back at the last few decades of American public schooling, they will surely identify an educational system where students' scores on annual accountability tests became, almost relentlessly, the prominent determiner of a school's success. But what if many of the tests currently used to evaluate our schools are inappropriate? If this is true, then many less-skilled teachers whose

---

[1] This chapter is adapted from an *Educational Leadership* article, "Standardized Tests: Purpose Is the Point," April 2016, 73(7), 44–49.

students score well on the wrong tests will not receive the professional support those teachers desperately need. Perhaps even worse, because the students taught by especially capable teachers might have earned low scores on the wrong tests, then many of those fine teachers will be urged to abandon effective instructional techniques that, according to students' test scores, appear to be flopping. The net effect of such misguided decisions, of course, is that massive numbers of students will end up receiving a lower quality education than they should. A central contention of this book is that many of the tests currently used to evaluate our schools are inappropriate.

PUBLICATION OF THE JOINT *STANDARDS*

Any worthwhile profession possesses one or more sets of "sacred scripture," that is, collections of profession-approved guidelines intended to govern the conduct of a given profession's members. In the case of educational testing, this influential document is the *Standards for Educational and Psychological Testing* published by the American Educational Research Association (2014). These standards, revised every decade or so, supply a set of well-vetted admonitions from the three national organizations most concerned with U.S. educational testing: namely, the American Educational Research Association (AERA), the American Psychological Association (APA), and the National Council on Measurement in Education (NCME). Frequently referred to as the "joint *Standards*" because of the three organizations that collaboratively sponsor their development, the most recently approved version of the joint *Standards* was published in July 2014.

The 2014 joint *Standards* are likely to have a major impact on U.S. educational testing because this document often plays a prominent role in courtroom litigation involving educational tests, such as cases centered on the use of students' test scores to evaluate teachers or schools. During the past several decades, for example, judicial authorities have often deferred to earlier versions of the joint *Standards* on the grounds that these recommendations constituted the best advice from our nation's most highly regarded educational measurement specialists. Such educational measurement specialists, incidentally, are often referred to as **psychometricians.** Documents that can sway juries, such as the joint *Standards,* of course, are likely to influence the evidence and arguments that litigants present in court.

For many years, and in several previous editions of the joint *Standards,* the most important feature of an educational test was the accuracy with which a test-based *interpretation* (or, if you prefer, a test-based *inference*) depicted a test-taker's covert capabilities, such as a student's mastery of a cognitive skill or a body of knowledge. Yet, for a number of years, increasingly large numbers of measurement specialists have also been clamoring for educational tests to be judged not only by the interpretation/accuracy stemming from test scores but also according to the *consequences* when those interpretations were actually implemented. Happily, the architects of the 2014 joint *Standards* joined the consequences of test-usage with the need to arrive at accurate purpose-based interpretations regarding what a particular test-taker's score means.

This important game-changing emphasis of the 2014 joint *Standards* calls for the accuracy of test scores to always be judged *"for proposed uses."* By blending the proposed *use* of a test with the need to arrive at accurate interpretations about a test-taker's performance, the writers of the 2014 joint *Standards* adroitly resolved how to infuse test-usage into the quest for accurate purpose-based interpretations.

HOW WE GOT HERE

For almost a full century, U.S. educational tests have been aimed at providing test users with *comparative-score interpretations.* Such comparisons were necessary so that the performance of a test-taker who scored at a particular level (in relation to the scores of previous test-takers constituting the test's "norm group") could be compared with other test-takers who had scored at different levels.

A major boost to America's comparatively oriented testing was seen during World War I when the *Army Alpha*, a group-administered mental ability test, was given to more than 1,750,000 Army recruits to identify those men who were most likely to succeed in officer-training programs. The *Alpha*, designed to measure recruits' verbal and quantitative cognitive abilities, was an **aptitude test**, that is, a test designed to predict test-takers' performances in a subsequent setting (in this instance, to predict recruits' success in an Army officer-training program). This substantial use of the *Alpha* was widely seen as a measurement success story, for the test proved remarkably effective in isolating the most intellectually able Army recruits via its comparative-score interpretation strategy.

Although the *Alpha* was an aptitude test, shortly after the conclusion of World War I, a number of educational **achievement tests** were published in this country. An example of such achievement exams was the initial edition of the now widely used, oft-revised *Stanford Achievement Tests* first published in 1923—not long after the close of World War I. These achievement tests were not intended to measure students' future success but, rather, tested students' mastery of particular subject-matter content, such as students' knowledge and skills in mathematics, language arts, or social studies. Clearly influenced by the *Alpha's* success, these rapidly emerging standardized achievement tests relied on the same test-development strategy embodied in building the *Army Alpha*, that is, a comparative-score interpretation approach. For almost one hundred years, such a comparative approach to educational testing has completely dominated assessment in our nation's schools.

Is there a need for tests to provide comparative score interpretations? Of course there is. In most settings where we find more applicants than the number of available openings, what's needed is a comparatively oriented measurement strategy so that we can identify the very best (or in some instances, the very worst) among a group of test-takers. Although the need to arrive at comparative-score interpretations among a group of test-takers can constitute a useful purpose of educational testing, it is not the *sole* purpose of educational testing.

Remember, the 2014 joint *Standards* stress the importance of arriving at accurate interpretations about test-takers *for a specific test use.* If an educational test is *not* intended for a purpose chiefly dependent on comparative-score interpretations, then the test's comparative virtues are largely irrelevant. What's needed today, therefore, is evidence regarding test quality that's focused on the *particular* purpose for which a test is to be used.

> If, as the 2014 joint *Standards* assert, the most important consideration in appraising an educational test is the degree to which the test yields accurate inferences related to the test's proposed purpose, then it seems obvious that we should abandon a century's worth of "one-size-fits-all" thinking about educational testing.

A DIFFERENCE-MAKING WAY OF CONSIDERING EDUCATIONAL TESTS

If, as the 2014 joint *Standards* assert, the most important consideration in appraising an educational test is the degree to which the test yields accurate inferences related to the test's proposed purpose, then it seems obvious that we should abandon a century's worth of "one-size-fits-all" thinking about educational testing. We should turn, instead, to a different way of conceptualizing tests according to the dominant educational purpose a test intends to accomplish. We can do so by adopting an approach to educational testing where the intended use of a test plays an unequivocally *dominant* role. We can refer to a measurement approach wherein tests are built and appraised according to this strategy as *purposeful educational assessment.*

Purposeful educational assessment requires the test's primary purpose to become *the overridingly important* factor in the creation of a test, and in the evaluation of that test. Such a profound shift in the importance of the test purpose will lead to key changes in the way we build educational tests and, once they have been built, in the way we judge their appropriateness for an intended use. Thus, test-developers and test-evaluators should no longer be able to "get by" merely by offering lip service endorsement of purpose-influenced assessment. Instead, they must provide persuasive *evidence* that educational tests truly do accomplish their intended uses.

With almost any tool, one can find multiple uses. A screwdriver, for example, in addition to its recognized screw-tightening and screw-loosening function, can also be used to poke holes in a can of tomato juice or auto oil. But the screwdriver's *primary* purpose, of course, is to insert and extract screws. An educational test also has a principal purpose, and it is conceptually head-clearing to isolate the most significant purpose for which we use an educational test. Figure 2.1 shows the three primary purposes of almost all educational tests, not necessarily presented in order of importance.

Figure 2.1   Three Primary Purposes of Educational Tests

- *Comparisons Among Test-Takers:* To compare students' test performances so that the score-based differences among individual students, or among groups of students, can be identified. The resultant comparisons often lead to the subsequent classification of students' scores either on a student-by-student basis or on a group-by-group basis.
- *Improvement of Ongoing Instruction and Learning:* To elicit evidence regarding students' current levels of learning so that informed decisions can be reached regarding what changes, if any, should be made in teachers' current instruction or in students' efforts to learn.

- *Evaluation of Instruction:* To determine the quality of an already completed set of instructional activities provided by a teacher, or by the staff of a particular school or district. Such evaluative appraisals usually judge the quality of fairly lengthy segments of instruction—sometimes lasting for a full school year.

Remembering that *one* of these three primary purposes must always be paramount in any application of purposeful educational assessment, let's briefly consider each of the three purposes in a bit more detail.

Comparisons among test-takers. One primary purpose of educational testing is assessing test-takers' performances so as to allow score-based comparisons. These comparisons can be made on a student-by-student basis, for example, when we calculate students' *percentile*-based status in relationship to that of other students in a norm group, such as when a high-scoring student's score is reported as being at the 96th percentile. Comparisons can also be made by assigning students to such qualitatively distinct categories as *advanced, proficient, basic,* or *below basic.*

To illustrate the diversity of score-based decisions when a test functions chiefly in a comparative fashion, we can think of choices that might be made about *individual* students such as grade-to-grade promotions for third-graders whose scores on a standardized reading test are used to signify readiness for fourth-grade reading. As an example of the decisions that can be linked to differences among test-classified student *groups,* we often see an entire school labeled as "under-performing" if too few of the school's students scored high enough on state accountability tests to "meet or exceed standards."

But what's important to recognize about comparison-focused testing is that any subsequent decisions made about test-takers—individually or grouped—are simply *applications* of testing—testing that already has a primary purpose. The primary function of comparison-focused educational tests is solely to *compare*. Once those test-based comparisons are made, we can employ a given educational test's comparisons for such applications as diploma-denying, award-giving, or even satisfying a governmental requirement to undertake annual accountability testing. But the *primary* purpose of comparison-focused educational testing is to do a solid job of contrasting the performances of those who were tested. Applications of students' test-compared status, of course, are numerous.

Improvement of ongoing instruction and learning. A second primary purpose of educational testing is to supply evidence capable of contributing either to improving instruction that teachers are currently providing to their students, or to improving how students themselves are currently trying to learn. This second purpose of instruction is integral to *formative assessment,* a measurement-strengthened instructional process whereby assessment-elicited evidence collected during an instructional sequence allows teachers, if necessary, to adjust their current instruction or allows students, if necessary, to adjust their current learning tactics. A test aimed at such a primary purpose can either supply educators with information about *groups* of students or with information about *individual* students. But whether aimed at groups of students or at solo students, the thrust of such testing is to engender more focused instruction that can better meet the needs of students.

As you will see in Chapter 8, rarely do large-scale standardized tests mesh well with this second instructionally focused purpose of educational testing. Typically, it is quite difficult to secure instructional insights from standardized tests that are administered only once a year, and usually at the end of the year, when students are moving on to a new teacher. For example, almost all truly effective applications of formative assessment rely on classroom assessments whose use can better coincide with what is being currently taught by a particular teacher.

Please note that this second, primary purpose of educational testing deals with the improvement of *ongoing* instruction and *ongoing* learning for the same students, not *future* instruction and learning for a different set of students. Future instruction, as you will now see, can best be improved by tests whose primary purpose is to evaluate instruction.

Evaluation of instruction. A third primary purpose of educational testing is to supply evidence for use in the evaluation of a set of instructional activities. Depending on the duration of the instructional activities being evaluated, this purpose of educational testing might be focused on a lengthy instructional segment, such as an academic year's worth of reading instruction or, in contrast, might deal with an abbreviated collection of instructional activities, such as those found in a teacher's implementation of a lesson to be carried out during several class periods.

Throughout history, as is true with all kinds of professionals, teachers have naturally wanted to know whether their efforts were effective. Yet, not until the passage of the Elementary and Secondary Education Act in 1965 (ESEA) were American educators formally directed by their federal government to collect evidence regarding the success of their instruction—in particular the effectiveness of those educational interventions that were federally supported. After ESEA's enactment, state-level recipients of a given year's federal funds supporting Program X were required to supply evaluative evidence that Program X had indeed been worth what it cost the nation's taxpayers.

Because appraising the caliber of an educational intervention is typically centered on determining how much students have actually learned, it was not surprising to see that most of an emerging set of 1960s educational evaluators (post-ESEA evaluators) employed the educational tests with which they were most familiar. That is, these novice educational evaluators were most conversant with students' test scores on off-the-shelf nationally standardized achievement tests then distributed by a half dozen major educational testing firms. And so it was that for more than a half-century, we have seen the evaluation of most U.S. educational interventions, particularly the largest of those interventions, determined chiefly by students' scores on nationally standardized achievement tests or, in some instances, by scores on state-developed replicas of those national tests.

This third primary purpose of educational testing, of course, is integral to educators' decisions about whether the instruction they provide for their students was successful. Because tests fulfilling this third primary purpose are intended to help educators tell whether their current instructional efforts are adequate, there is rarely a need for particularization at the level of the individual student. Thus, when school district officials, or individual teachers, are trying to decide whether their "this year's" instructional program should be altered for "next year's" instruction, most evaluation-informed decisions will be based on group-aggregated data.

Looking back at the use of high-stakes educational tests during the past half-century, one is struck by the increasingly prevalent use of evidence from those tests to indicate that our nation's schools are "less effective than they ought to be." Interestingly, in almost all of those evaluation-focused applications of a test's results, the tests used were not demonstrated to be suitable for this evaluative function. More often than not, a *comparatively* focused test was employed in an *evaluative* role—even though the test was neither developed for, nor evaluated for, such an evaluative function.

Well, if purposeful educational testing does not make an *actual* difference in the way tests are developed and evaluated, then this three-category distinction, depicted graphically in Figure 2.2, is surely a contrast without consequence.

WHAT'S THE DECISION AT ISSUE?

One of the best ways to determine an educational test's primary purpose is to *identify the decision to be*

Figure 2.2 Three Primary Purposes of Educational Testing

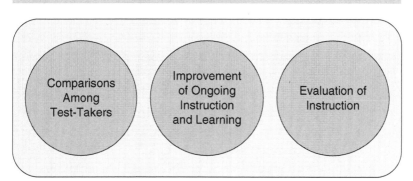

made based on test-takers' performances. Surely there is a decision in the offing that's dependent on students' scores. If you can isolate this decision, then the test's purpose almost always becomes instantly apparent. But is this splitting of educational testing into three arenas simply a theoretical quest for accurate test-labeling, or are other consequences involved?

Well, if purposeful educational testing does not make an *actual* difference in the way tests are developed and evaluated, then this three-category distinction, depicted graphically in Figure 2.2, is surely a contrast without consequence. To have the necessary impact on the way educational tests are actually built and evaluated, a purposeful assessment approach must—from the earliest conceptualizing of what needs to be done—influence every major decision to be made about an educational test.

To illustrate, if a test is being built to improve ongoing teaching and learning, then it is imperative that the test's builders do not attempt to measure students' mastery of too many curricular targets. Trying to measure too many curricular targets makes it impossible to assess mastery of particular targets with enough items to provide sufficiently accurate per-target estimates of students' mastery status. If, for example, a state's official curricular aims for fifth-grade mathematics consist of more than forty distinct mathematical skills, then trying to measure students' mastery of all those skills leads to only one or two items per skill—too few to supply instructionally diagnostic information. In most settings, what's sought curricularly for a state's students is determined by content specialists, such as a group of approximately thirty or so seasoned math teachers. And when content specialists convene in order to identify what students should learn, they almost always want students to learn everything!

Thus, rather than meekly accepting a direction to measure too many curricular targets, a test's builders must, from the very outset, resist ill-conceived demands that too much be measured. *Prioritization* of proposed assessment targets can allow the identification of a manageable number of to-be-measured assessment targets that can, as a consequence, actually contribute to improved instruction.

The most important recognition regarding a purposeful assessment strategy's three-purpose focus is that attention to purpose must be paramount. The primary purpose of a particular educational test should—from the very get-go—*dominate* the decision making of those who build a test as well as those who evaluate that test. This purpose-domination is essentially absent from America's educational testing.

Takeaway Time

This second chapter deals with the overriding importance of *purpose* when educational tests are built, and thereafter evaluated. A prominent emphasis of the 2014 joint *Standards* calling for clear, early on explication of an educational test's primary purpose spurred the isolation of the three dominant educational test purposes as the chapter's chief understanding. In later chapters, you will learn how these three differences in purpose influence the construction and the subsequent appraisal of educational tests.

> **Purposeful Educational Testing:** *The construction and evaluation of educational tests should be profoundly influenced by one of the three primary purposes of such testing, namely, (1) comparisons among test-takers, (2) improvement of ongoing instruction and learning, or (3) evaluation of instruction.*

As you complete the remaining chapters in the book, you will find that this three-prism view of educational assessment's purposes often leads to serious differences in how tests ought to be constructed and, once built, how they should be evaluated. Is it not reasonable for a person's activities to be guided by that person's purpose? Of course it is. Accordingly, chalk up another mark in your mental "Common-Sense Assessment" column!

3

Behind Standardized Testing's Cloudy Curtain

Most educators understand the fundamentals of what goes on when a teacher-made test is born, because at some point in their careers most educators have been obliged to crank out such tests. Indeed, most of today's experienced teachers have personally constructed hundreds—if not thousands—of tests for their own students. There's little mystery about the creation of classroom tests because, by definition, teacher-made tests are made by teachers.

Of course, teachers vary in the skills they use to generate a classroom test. Surely, not all teacher-made tests are created equal—at least not equal in quality. Nonetheless, there's a widespread recognition among educators regarding the chief activities required when teachers gin up their own classroom tests. Numerous variations exist among such tests. For instance, there are differences in test lengths, item types, and what's being measured. Even so, almost all educators know the same general steps to follow when building classroom tests.

Although most educators are comfortably conversant with the nuts and bolts involved in creating classroom tests, such conversance is absent when it comes to their understanding of how *standardized* tests are constructed. In fact, most teachers are altogether uninformed about the building of such large-scale tests as the annual accountability exams a particular state's students are required to take, or the national college aptitude exams that many high-school students complete annually. To most educators, even those who are skilled builders of their own classroom tests, what goes on behind the scenes when standardized tests are built is a mystery. But it shouldn't be.

Far too many teachers and school administrators, because they are unfamiliar with the procedures employed when large-scale standardized tests are developed, mistakenly assume that the construction or the critiquing of such tests is beyond them. That is, such educators believe that decisions regarding standardized tests should be left only to those who are bona fide assessment specialists. Educators might conclude that it is difficult to comment sensibly on what they do not comprehend. As a consequence, most educators remain oblivious of what lurks behind the "curtain" of standardized test construction and defer to whatever has been hatched by the architects of standardized educational tests.

And who are these "architects" of standardized achievement tests? In the preceding chapter, the term *psychometrician* was used to describe a measurement expert, yet such experts usually focus their efforts on the quantitative side of test-building, such as how to statistically equate two different forms of the same test so that both forms present an essentially identical challenge to test-takers. In addition to psychometricians, however, a number of other specialists are involved in the creation of standardized tests—for instance, the content specialists who initially identify the knowledge and skills to be assessed, then monitor the accuracy of the items being built to assess such content. Then, of course, there are the folks who write the actual items themselves. In some cases a standardized test's items are authored by writers employed by the test-development firm that's constructing the test. In other instances, classroom teachers are recruited, trained, and then end up generating most of a standardized test's items. In short, we usually find that a standardized educational test is created by a cadre of diverse assessment specialists—especially a test being used to make important decisions about test-takers or those who educate them.

What's most worrisome about this state of affairs is that the nation's educators, and almost everyone else, assume that those who build and evaluate standardized tests are doing it correctly. Hopefully, this book will squeeze some of the helium out of that unwarranted balloon.

As the alluring subtitle of this book alleges, the aspiration of the book is aimed at *Demystifying the Tools That Shape Our Schools.* This subtitle (which, I confess, required several days' worth of back-and-forth rewording on my part) attempts to communicate two important points. The first is that educational testing—particularly large-scale standardized testing—is seen as intimidating and mysterious by most educators. Through the years, I've spent sufficient time talking with all sorts of teachers and administrators to know this is true. Indeed, for a number of years I taught an introductory graduate course about educational testing, and I was nearly required to hand out tranquilizer pills as my students entered the classroom. Put plainly, many educators are just plain scared of anything associated with really "important" educational assessment simply because they don't know how it is that significant educational tests are built. The subtitle's second stressed point is that educational tests are remarkably influential in currently determining what transpires in the nation's classrooms: today's tests "shape our schools."

High Stakes and Tomato Plants

One of the more delightful bumper stickers that I've ever run into—and this was a couple of decades ago, when standardized tests first began to be used to make important decisions—was the following: "High stakes should be used for tomato plants, not tests." The creators of that bumper sticker were relying on a gardening metaphor to register opposition against our nation's increasing reliance on students' test scores when making important decisions about students, teachers, administrators, and our schools in general.

When significant contingencies are riding on the way test scores turn out, it is not surprising to learn that whatever is tested by such high-consequence tests will almost always end up being stressed instructionally by teachers. The reason is all too obvious. Except for a handful of psychotics, all of us want to do well whenever we tackle a task. I'm assuming that you want to understand what you're reading in this book, and I want to write a book well so that it is easy for you to understand stuff about educational testing. We all want to do well because our human nature shrieks out for us to perform as successfully as we can. Thus, because our educational systems are centered on the enhancement of students' learning, and because the evidence of students' learning is served up to us most directly in the form of students' test performances, it is not surprising that many educators engage in instructional activities they believe will improve students' test scores. It's just the way humans are built.

But when we split the educational testing world into two halves, namely, teacher-made classroom assessments and externally imposed standardized assessments, one of those two halves is clearly associated with far higher stakes than is the other. Because it is widely believed that classroom tests are not as carefully developed as standardized tests, and because it is feared by some critics that teachers might not be as scrupulous in scoring students' classroom-test performances as occurs in the scoring of students' standardized-test efforts, externally imposed standardized tests are seen as the real "truth-telling" measurements. Thus, readers of this book need to be reasonably familiar with how such tests are developed.

Same Script: More Bells, More Whistles

I'm hoping to convince you in the remainder of this chapter that, if you understand the main steps in the creation of a teacher-made classroom test, you will also understand the nature of what goes on when standardized educational tests are developed. The chief differences are that when standardized tests are constructed, because of the higher stakes often linked to test-takers' performances on such exams, the steps taken to generate these tests are typically more carefully considered and more formally documented.

First, let's agree on the meaning of a few terms that we'll be using during this brief dip into test construction. First off, although I've used the term a few times already, what exactly is a standardized test? A *standardized test is a test that's administered, scored, and interpreted in a consistent, predetermined manner.* Typically, standardized tests are built and administered by for-profit companies such as Pearson Assessment or by not-for-profit organizations such as the Educational Testing Service. Other common sources of standardized tests are state departments of education, which are often assisted by external contractors. Standardized tests, if they are "administered, scored, and interpreted in a consistent predetermined manner," could conceivably be built even by a school district, a school's staff, or during a summer vacation by a seriously bored teacher.

Standardized tests are usually divided into two categories, standardized *aptitude* tests and standardized *achievement* tests. The function of aptitude tests is to predict a test-taker's likelihood of success in some future setting—such as was the purpose of the World War I *Army Alpha* that predicted Army recruits' potential success in officer-training programs. A common example of an aptitude test these days is the SAT or the ACT, since they are intended to forecast how successful high-school students will be, grade-wise, when they get into college. In contrast, an achievement test attempts to measure the knowledge and/or skills that a student possesses. So, for example, if a state's educational policymakers have identified a dozen mathematical skills that state officials wish all students to possess as a consequence of their education, then a standardized achievement test could be used to determine each student's mastery of those mathematical skills.

Building Classroom Assessments:
A Bare Bones Approach

Because this chapter centers on the proposition that the creation of standardized tests—either achievement tests or aptitude tests—is nothing more than a super-deluxe version of how most teachers crank out their own classroom assessments, let's take a look at what most teachers do when they build a classroom test. Recalling Chapter 2's contention that three primary purposes account for practically all of educational testing, which of these three measurement missions do most teachers have in mind when they set out to build their own classroom tests—or when they use a classroom test developed by others (for instance, tests created by a textbook publisher or by a commercial testing firm)?

Well, if a teacher wanted to determine the quality of the teacher's own instructional activities, such as might be required for a school district's teacher-appraisal system, then the function of a test to be built would clearly be *evaluation*. If, on the other hand, a teacher were using a classroom test chiefly to help the teacher identify which parts of an ongoing instructional program needed to be modified to be more effective, then the function of the test would surely be *instructional*. Finally, if a teacher's dominant purpose for a classroom test were to rank students' achievement levels so that grades could be dispensed according to students' relative standings, then the assessment function of such a test would be *comparative*. Let's see how classroom tests are built in accordance with a teacher's assessment purpose.

Step 1: Purpose determination. The first step in building a classroom assessment calls for the teacher to identify the primary purpose of the classroom test. For many teachers—perhaps for *most* teachers—this is to compare students' relative mastery of what's being measured so as to inform a teacher's awarding of grades. Those grades could be associated with short-duration instructional units or with longer-term instructional activities, such as what was instructionally covered during an entire school year. If you were to consult any introductory textbook dealing with classroom assessment (I find myself magnetically drawn to a textbook that I wrote myself [Popham, 2017], but a number of friends and colleagues have also written first-rate classroom assessment textbooks, for instance, Stiggins & Chappuis, 2012, and Nitko & Brookhart, 2014), you will find that the ways a test's items are built depends heavily on the primary purpose of the test being built. To illustrate, if the function of a teacher's end-of-course final examination is to compare students' achievement so that grades could be dispensed according to those students' relative achievement levels, then the items to be used in a test should maximize the degree of *score-spread* among students. Put simply, when using test results to grade students, too much "bunching up" of students who have identical or similar scores makes it tough, for grading purposes, to accurately differentiate among those students. The more spread out that students' scores are, the more fine-grained can be the comparisons and, as a result, the more defensible will be a teacher's decisions regarding the allocation of grades.

Had the teacher's primary purpose for a classroom test been either instructional or evaluative, then key differences would exist in the generation of the test's items. The chief point here is that, to accomplish different primary purposes, different ways exist for constructing a test's items and, if those items need to be fixed so they can function more appropriately, for subsequently improving the items.

Step 2: Content selection. After determining a classroom test's primary purpose, the next step is identifying the knowledge and/or skills to be assessed by the test. This seemingly simple second step is far more daunting than teachers typically recognize. When an often too vague curricular aim is being *operationalized,* that is, when a curricular aim (also called *"content standard," "goal," "learning outcome,"* or *"instructional target"*) is being spelled out so that we better understand what it really calls for when students have mastered it, teachers often have trouble defining how to assess it. As any teacher who has undertaken this second step of test construction can tell you, it is far easier to blather about somewhat general curricular targets than it is to explicate with genuine precision what sorts of items will indicate whether a student has, in fact, attained a squishy curricular aspiration.

These days, educators often characterize the level of cognitive challenge that's embodied by an item as its **depth of knowledge (DOK)** to indicate whether a classroom test's items represent a sufficiently demanding task for students. One widely used depth of knowledge continuum ranges from "Recall and Reproduction" (such as memorized information) up to "Skills and Concepts"

> If the test has a dominant purpose of supplying instructional guidance, then care must be taken not to bite off too much content to measure.

(such as multiplying fractions or distinguishing facts from opinions) up to "Short-Term Strategic Thinking" (such as designing an experiment) and, finally, up to "Extended Thinking" (such as synthesizing information from diverse sources). In earlier years, when categorizing the cognitive demands of curricular aims, most educators relied on a six-level system developed by Benjamin Bloom and colleagues in 1956. Bloom's *Taxonomy of Educational Objectives* started at the low end with "Knowledge," then headed higher on the cognition highway with "Comprehension," "Application," "Analysis," "Synthesis," and ended up at the top with "Evaluation."

Finally, as indicated above, a classroom test's primary purpose plays a prominent role in choosing the content for such a test. If the test's dominant purpose is to supply instructional guidance, then care must be taken not to bite off too much content to measure.

Usually, a number of items are needed to assess students' mastery of each of the curricular aims to measure—and experienced teachers can typically estimate approximately how many items are required to help determine students' mastery of different aims. Accordingly, trying to measure too many curricular aims essentially precludes the use of sufficient items per aim—because the test would then be too long. As always, we see in this second step that a test's primary assessment purpose really dominates so many aspects of test development.

Step 3: Item construction/revision. The third and final step in development of a classroom test requires a teacher to build (or select from an existing item pool) the items that permit an inference to be drawn regarding a student's status in relation to the test's purpose. This score-based inference about a student, or, perhaps about a whole group of students, should lead to the reason this whole three-step sequence was carried out in the first place, namely, to a *decision*. This decision, of course, depends on the purpose and use for the test.

You will note that this third step in creating classroom tests calls for the construction of a test's items or the subsequent revision of those items. Happily, some teachers have the energy to both construct a classroom test's items and to revise those items that require improvement. Regrettably, many busy teachers simply do not have the time or the zeal to spiffy up a set of already built items. Such item revision, however, almost always improves a test's quality.

As indicated previously, when deciding what sorts of items contribute most to a teacher's valid inference about students' mastery of curricular aims measured by a classroom test, almost any textbook dealing with the basics of classroom assessment can provide a wide range of diverse item types to consider, for example, multiple-choice items and short-response questions. At this stage of the test-development enterprise, here's where a teacher's good sense needs to run the item-creation show.

There is no surefire, never-wrong way to arrive at these "what items and how many" decisions. Teachers simply have to do the best they can to make such choices and be willing to revise based on the students' responses. And the more familiar a teacher is with a wide range of item-type options, and with ways of making revisions to improve those items, the better.

Figure 3.1 is a representation of the three-step sequence just described for building a classroom assessment. As noted above—when this three-step model was being described—many teachers typically move rather rapidly through such a test-building approach, often using short-cut mental machinations to arrive at what they regard as an acceptable classroom test. Rarely do teachers enlist the aid of colleagues or supervisors in the assembly of such tests and rarely do they document the procedures they employed in building their own tests. Rarely do teachers actually evaluate their classroom tests once those tests have been built.

Figure 3.1   A Three-Step Test Development Process

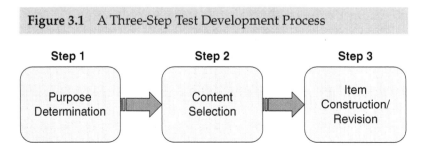

Step 1	Step 2	Step 3
Purpose Determination	Content Selection	Item Construction/ Revision

Standardized Test Development: More Care, More Documentation

The three-step process described above is precisely what goes on behind the curtains when the developers of standardized tests generate the assessment devices often destined to become high-stakes assessment instruments. There are only two important differences involved, namely, (1) the care going into the test-development and test-revision operations and (2) the level of documentation taking place as a test is being built and improved. Although some of these test-building and test-honing practices for standardized tests are carried out using fairly fancy terminology and techniques, at their root they are essentially equivalent to what goes on when teachers develop their own classroom tests.

To illustrate, when the primary purpose is initially being chosen for an important standardized test's measurement mission, it is necessary for those who are creating the test to spell out, as unequivocally as possible, what's going to be done with the test's results. Any open deliberations regarding a test's chief purpose, as well as the decisions to be informed by a test's results, should include representatives of all concerned constituencies and should lead to a transparent spell-out of the decisions that will be riding on a test's results.

Similarly, when both Step 2, Content Selection, and Step 3, Item Construction/Revision are being carried out for a standardized test, not only should considerable care be given to choosing the participants who will take part in such activities but attention should also be given to the ways in which those participants are supposed to carry out their work. When a high-stakes standardized test is being built, all important activities in the development process should be carefully—even

> Yet, if many measurement specialists are required—possibly under Taser threat—to describe their standardized test-building in truly understandable terms, *they can do so.*

extra-carefully—documented. Documentation of the ways in which test-development activities are carried out will typically help others evaluate whether a test has achieved its primary purpose.

Whether it's an achievement tests or an aptitude test, the people engaged in developing a test and in documenting their efforts are almost always following the simple three-step strategy we saw when teachers crank out their own tests. Sure, the measurement-savvy folks involved in the generation of standardized tests often employ a ton of technical lingo— terms less comprehensible to normal humans. Yet, if many measurement specialists are required—possibly under Taser threat—to describe their standardized test-building in truly understandable terms, *they can do so.*

Indeed, once we strip away such specialists' technical vocabulary and dig into the heart of properly described test-development, you'll find that what went on is really very "old hat" after all.

TAKEAWAY TIME

In this chapter, a case has been made that the straightforward three-step approach most teachers employ when they create their own classroom tests is fundamentally what goes on when psychometricans fashion a standardized educational test. The reason that so few people understand what takes place during the birthing of standardized tests is the absence of plain-language explanations of what measurement specialists are up to. If a measurement expert cannot clearly describe—in jargon-free terms—what takes place when a particular standardized test is built and polished, perhaps that measurement expert really does not understand what transpired.

Standardized Test Development. *Although essentially identical to the procedures used when teacher-made classroom tests are built, the development of standardized assessments relies on particularly careful test-building and more complete—yet plain-language explainable—documentation of purpose determination, content selection, and item construction/revision.*

What's going on when standardized tests are constructed is essentially identical to what goes on when teachers construct their own classroom tests. With standardized tests, particularly with high-stakes ones, far greater care goes into the process and its documentation. That process, however, should *always* be explainable in comprehensible language by those involved. Although, when truly significant standardized educational tests are being built or evaluated, it's almost always the case that more whistles and frills are added to procedures that, at their roots, are disarmingly simple and sensible. This chapter attempts to heighten your comfort in dealing with the remaining set of assessment issues addressed in later chapters. Candidly, I don't want you to be put off in your understanding of what's going on in those chapters because you think the high-stakes versions of educational testing—those involving standardized tests—are beyond you. As I hope you now see, they really aren't.

4

Validity

The Crux of the Caper

Most authors are reluctant to supply along-the-way commentaries on their own writing. Ordinarily, I am too. But I'm making an exception in this instance because I want you to recognize that this chapter about *validity* is, hands down, the most important chapter in the entire book. If *I* don't do a solid job of explaining what validity is, or—assuming that my explanation is okay—if *you* don't do a solid job in grasping what the chapter says, you're certain to be seriously limited in your overall understanding of what educational assessment is all about. Accordingly, we *both* have a job to do.

"Valid Tests" Don't Exist!

Let's get under way by isolating the reason that teachers test their students at all. Put plainly, teachers test kids because teachers can't see what's going on inside kids' heads. That's right, teachers frequently need to get a fix on a student's knowledge—such as how well a student has memorized a collection of punctuation rules—or to estimate a student's mastery of a cognitive skill—such as how successfully a student is able to multiply pairs of triple-digit numbers. But a student's knowledge and a student's skills are *covert*, they simply can't be seen, no matter how closely a teacher looks—even with the aid of a microscope or a ritzy magnetic resonance imaging (MRI) machine.

Because, for instructional reasons, teachers often need to identify students' knowledge and skills when devising plans to instruct those students, teachers must construct educational tests that require students to supply *overt* behavior in the form of their responses to a test's items. These overt responses permit teachers to arrive at conclusions regarding what it is that students know and can do. Whether the test that's being used is a traditional paper-and-pencil exam or requires actual performance, such as when a student in a music class must play a violin, teachers employ students' *overt* responses to a test's items in order to arrive at a conclusion regarding a student's *covert* status with respect to whatever was measured.

For example, if a seventh-grade student completes an essay-writing test where the student composes two simply dazzling descriptive essays, the teacher might reasonably conclude that the seventh grader is a good writer of descriptive essays. Similarly, if a high-school student in a social studies course writes, from scratch, a cracking good account of the key steps in how a person is elected to the U.S. presidency, a teacher could then sensibly conclude that the student understands how America's presidential-election process works.

As you will soon see, when describing the nature of assessment validity, two terms are often employed, namely, an **inference** and an **interpretation**. The terms are interchangeable. Both of these labels refer to a reasoned conclusion—based on test-corralled evidence—regarding a test-taker's unseen knowledge and/or skills. Some writers prefer to use the label *interpretation*; others prefer *inference*. It's really your choice—as long as you remember that we are absolutely obliged to rely on a student's overt responses to a test in order to arrive at a conclusion (that is, an interpretation or an inference) about the student's covert status regarding the knowledge and/or skills being measured.

In Chapter 1's description of the influential nature of the 2014 *Standards for Educational and Psychological Testing*, you saw that the overriding importance of assessment validity is crisply described and unequivocally clear:

> Validity hinges on whether a score-based inference is both *accurate* and also *contributes to the accomplishment of a particular test's purpose.*

> Validity refers to the degree to which evidence and theory support the interpretations of test scores for proposed uses of tests. Validity is, therefore, the most fundamental consideration in developing tests and evaluating tests. (AERA, 2014, p. 11)

Please notice in this definition that the degree of validity hinges on the accuracy of score interpretations "for proposed uses of tests." The 2014 joint *Standards* emphasize, therefore, that not only must a score-based inference about a student's covert status be *accurate,* but there must also be evidence on hand supporting the use of such an inference *for the particular purpose* for which a test is being used. Validity, thus, is not a label that should be applied to a test itself. There is no such thing as a "valid test," nor is there an "invalid test." Tests aren't valid or invalid. Validity hinges on whether a score-based inference is both *accurate* and also *contributes to the accomplishment of a particular test's purpose.*

When we collect validation evidence for an educational test, we then use such evidence as part of *a validity argument* supporting a score-based inference's contribution to a test's primary purpose. Assessment validity centers on the strength of an argument regarding a test's *interpretive accuracy* and also its *fitness for purpose.* There is no numerically determined On-Off switch when we establish assessment validity. Rather, when using an educational test, validity flows from human judgment about the persuasiveness of a particular validity argument and the evidence on which that argument has been fashioned.

This is why there is genuine danger in anyone's labeling a test itself as "valid." You see, once a test gets a "valid" label slapped on it, then far too many people start believing that whatever scores such a test spits out are, themselves, valid (accurate) and useful. This belief is frequently mistaken.

You now know that when anyone utters the phrase, "a valid test," they are making a mistake regarding the very most important concept in the field of educational testing. What they may be doing, of course, is using a loose-language short-cut to convey the notion that "evidence exists to support an interpretation that test-takers' scores on this test are not only accurate, but also consistent with the intended use of this test." Accordingly, on hearing someone utter the phrase, "a valid test," it is not recommended that you fire off an on-the-spot, expletive-laden correction at the utterer. Nonetheless, conjuring up at least a mildly condescending sneer on your part seems altogether appropriate.

ESSENTIALS OF THE VALIDATION PROCESS

Clear-headedness about assessment validity is a necessary but not sufficient condition for smooth sailing through the remaining chapters of this charming plot-free book. Accordingly, I've tried to present in Figure 4.1 a graphic representation of what goes on when someone tries to assemble a validity argument for an educational test.

Will those who develop *high-stakes* educational tests typically go to the trouble of actually following through with the three steps portrayed in Figure 4.1? Yes, they will. These days, because the decisions linked to the results of high-stakes tests often have serious consequences, those who construct high-stakes tests would be ninnies not to do what's represented in Figure 4.1. Typically, each time a high-stakes test is constructed, those who construct it will prepare a test-development technical report seriously addressing the topic of assessment validity. For example, a written argument is typically provided in which an evidence-based analysis, hopefully persuasive, is set forth supporting the accuracy of a test's score-based inferences as well as the consonance of those inferences with a test's primary purpose.

As you can see in Figure 4.1, the first step in the validation process is focused on identifying and assembling evidence bearing on the *accuracy* of a test-taker's inferred status regarding what's being measured. Incidentally, when assessment specialists refer to a "test-based inference," they are not necessarily focusing only on the number of correct answers a student gets on a traditional paper-and-pencil test. When a student in a speech class delivers a required impromptu speech, and receives a certain number of points based on the teacher's evaluative use of a ***rubric***, that is, a scoring guide, then this point-total also is regarded as the student's "score." After collecting and assembling the Step 1 evidence regarding a score's accuracy, additional evidence is then collected in Step 2 regarding the degree to which a test-taker's score appropriately contributes to accomplishing the test's primary purpose. Finally, in Step 3, those two sets of evidence—

Figure 4.1   Required Steps in the Building of an Educational Test's Validity Argument

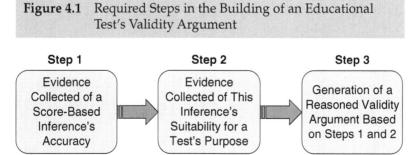

Step 1	Step 2	Step 3
Evidence Collected of a Score-Based Inference's Accuracy	Evidence Collected of This Inference's Suitability for a Test's Purpose	Generation of a Reasoned Validity Argument Based on Steps 1 and 2

the "inference-accuracy" evidence and the "purpose-accomplishment" evidence—are woven together in a validity argument that enables someone to reach a judgment regarding a test's suitability.

What about classroom teachers? Do they typically carry through with a multi-step validation effort such as that presented in Figure 4.1? Well, as you might guess, most teachers are far too busy to lavish such validation attention on their own teacher-made tests. Nonetheless, the same kind of purpose-focused validation activity can apply to the creation of classroom tests as it does to the building of high-stakes standardized tests. What we can hope for from classroom teachers is that, for at least their most significant teacher-made tests, teachers *mentally* engage in some serious thinking along the lines depicted in Figure 4.1. Teacher-made tests created by teachers who at least "think through" such validation steps will, almost always, turn out to be better tests than those produced less thoughtfully.

It is particularly important to recognize that what's going on throughout the entire collection and presentation of validity evidence is an application of *human judgment*. For example, judgments must be made about which sorts of evidence will most appropriately support the accuracy of a score-based inference about a test-taker. To illustrate, if a brand new district-developed test has been built to measure middle-school students' "close-reading" skills in order for the district's teachers to instructionally improve their students' close-reading capabilities, what sorts of *evidence* will be supportive of interpretations that students who scored high on the new test were skilled close-readers, whereas low-scoring students were unskilled close-readers?

Let's suppose there is pretty convincing evidence that test-based inferences about middle-schoolers' close-reading skills are apt to be reasonably accurate. We turn to the purpose of the new close-reading test, which is to help teachers improve students' close-reading skills. Then a judgment must be made regarding what sorts of evidence will support the use of test-based interpretations and consequent instructional actions to *improve* students' close-reading skills. It is one thing to conclude that accurate inferences can be based on students' test scores, but it is quite another to determine that those inferences actually contribute to the reason the test is being used.

Finally, with the "inference-accuracy" evidence and the "purpose-accomplishment" evidence at hand, a validation argument must then be fashioned so that those considering the use of a test's results can arrive at a final judgment regarding the appropriateness of this use. In essence, as seen previously in Figure 4.1, the following three-step set of judgments must be employed when implementing the validation process for educational tests:

Inference-Accuracy Evidence → Fitness-for-Purpose Evidence → Validity Argument

But who does this validation-related judging?

THE VALIDATION VOYAGE

Can we expect busy classroom teachers to expend serious segments of their workdays to carrying out thoughtful analyses of available assessment evidence? Can we expect school board members or elected legislators to do so? Would it be likely that everyday citizens or the parents of students would have the know-how or the energy to undertake a thoughtful validation effort? The correct answer to all three of these questions is an unequivocal negative.

Where, then, will these needed validation analyses come from? How can we arrive at defensible judgments regarding whether a test's ability to yield accurate score-based interpretations meshes appropriately with the test's chief purpose? Without a compelling validity argument, we should be thoroughly uncertain about whether to use a test's results to achieve the test's intended purpose.

> If you enlist the consultative services of a measurement specialist whose validity explanations are enshrouded by jargon-laden opacity, then you need to find a different measurement specialist.

But we've seen that, as a practical matter, many individuals who really need to understand an educational test's quality are often too busy or insufficiently conversant with the test-validation process to reach a judgment about assessment validity. Although every reader of this book *could* learn how to carry out assessment validation efforts, few readers will wish—quite sensibly in my view—to put forth the necessary effort to do so.

I've put a fair amount of worried thinking into addressing this problem, and I've concluded that there's only one realistic source of *understandable* validity analyses for educational tests. We must enlist the explanatory services of knowledgeable assessment experts or measurement specialists who can explain the relevant evidence and validation argument for a particular test so that *such a plain-language explanation can be understood* by the members of any concerned, assessment-knowledgeable constituency. Actually, when I say members of "any concerned, assessment-knowledgeable constituency," I'm thinking of folks just like you—once you've finished this book.

Not all measurement specialists are up to the challenge of supplying truly lucid explanations of the assessment validation process, but if you enlist the consultative services of a measurement specialist whose validity explanations are enshrouded by jargon-laden opacity, then you need to find a different measurement specialist.

A reasonable-fee assessment expert can usually be hired by any group of interested individuals, such as members of a district school board, a school's Parent-Teacher Association, or a state's teachers' or administrators' associations. Such a measurement specialist's task, simply put, is to provide plain-language explanations of any existing evidence-based validity argument in support of a particular test's use. If the individuals who hired this assessment consultant understand the chief points in the book that you're currently reading, those folks will usually be able to judge whether the validity argument that's being described by a for-hire testing expert is sufficiently persuasive.

I've been arguing, since you began flipping this book's pages, that the fundamental concepts and procedures of educational testing are sufficiently understandable so anyone— anyone—can comprehend them. It's really true. What this particular truth implies, however, is that if a competent assessment expert is called on to lay out the important elements of a validity argument that's related to a particular test—to lay it out so clearly that it is understandable to a non-expert, then a truly *competent* assessment expert will be able to do so.

I believe this is the only way to hop the "too technical" hurdle when dealing with educational tests. Whether you're a member of a state school board, a superintendent of a school district, or the vice president of a district Parent-Teacher Association, if you want to know whether an educational test that you're using (or are considering using) is up to snuff, you need to hire a competent assessment consultant. Such a consultant must spell out for you, in language you can easily understand, the degree to which an evidence-based validity argument supports the intended use of a test.

A validity argument is much like the closing argument an attorney presents to a jury at the close of a trial. That's because a competent assessment expert should be able to identify the most pertinent evidence supporting score-based inferences and the use of those inferences to achieve the test's purpose. Then, just as a jury must mull a lawyer's arguments to arrive at a verdict, a test's users must also do some mulling to reach a judgment about assessment validity. While doing so, judgments about the suitability of a test invariably stem not from mysterious statistical gyrations but, rather, from the application of good old common sense.

GRIST FOR THE VALIDATION MILL

What sorts of evidence must be trotted out to indicate the suitability of an educational test? Personally, I find that when I clamber into the validation sandbox, my first activity is to isolate, in super-clear fashion, the purpose for the test under consideration. More specifically, I try to identify the specific decision(s) riding on a student's test scores. Typically, this helps me isolate the score-based inference to be made—that is, the score-based interpretation about a student that will, in turn, lead to an interpretation-based decision. Next, I try to identify the sort of inference-accuracy evidence and the sort of purpose-accomplishment evidence that will form the heart of a subsequent validity argument. Let's close out this chapter about validity by dealing with what I personally regard as the most profoundly *invalid* use of America's educational testing.

> The vast majority of educational tests we currently employ to evaluate instructional quality are unequivocally unfit for this function.

If the purpose of an educational test is to evaluate instructional quality, such as evaluating the success of instruction at a district's schools, I'd want to see evidence that the test possessed *instructional sensitivity.* That is, I'd be looking for persuasive evidence indicating whether the test could distinguish between well taught and poorly taught students. Such evidence might have been collected *judgmentally* during the development of the test by requiring experienced teachers to render a series of item-by-item judgments about each item's ability to discriminate between effectively taught and ineffectively taught students. Such evidence might also be garnered *empirically* when a test's items were initially tried out by comparing the per-item performances of students taught by exceptionally talented versus markedly less talented teachers. Items that failed to perform in the predicted manner by students who were taught by these two disparate groups of teachers would be scrutinized again to see, for instance, if performance on an item seemed more dependent on students' socioeconomic status than on the caliber of the instruction they had received.

To reiterate a contention that can't be reiterated too much these days, if an educational test is to be employed evaluatively, it simply *must* be accompanied by evidence (judgmental, empirical, or both of these) regarding the test's instructional sensitivity. If there's no compelling evidence that the test can differentiate between effective and ineffective instruction, then it should never be used to evaluate the instruction provided by individual teachers or by groups of teachers. Absent persuasive evidence of an evaluative test's instructional sensitivity, any resulting inferences about instructional sensitivity are completely suspect. The vast majority of educational tests we currently employ to evaluate instructional quality are unequivocally unfit for this function.

Takeaway Time

Early in this chapter you were battered with proclamations regarding the importance of validity in educational testing and the need to regard validation not as an attribute of a test itself but, rather, as a function of the accuracy of a score-based inference in relation to the primary purpose of an educational test. Evidence regarding the accuracy of score-based interpretations and the contribution of students' test performances to the accomplishment of a test's chief purpose should then be blended into a judgmentally fashioned validity argument.

Although the generation, "from scratch," of an evidence-based validity argument is typically well beyond the resources of many individuals or groups, it was recommended that if one possesses a familiarity with the central notions of educational testing, such as those described in this book, it often makes sense to enlist the aid of an assessment-skilled consultant who would be charged with explaining—in plain-language clarity—what kind of evidence-based validation argument had been provided for a test under consideration.

Assessment Validation. *Assessment validation, the most significant process in all of educational testing, culminates in the creation of a validity argument based on evidence of both the inference accuracy and the contribution of a test to the accomplishment of the chief purpose for which the test is used.*

As always, in an effort to keep this chapter's validity caper complication-free, you can simply recall that assessment validity calls for an educational test to be accompanied by evidence about the accuracy of score-based inferences and evidence of the contribution of those inferences to the achievement of a test's purpose. Really, this is all there is to it.

5

Reliability

Considering Consistency in Inconsistent Containers

S ome things just naturally go together. For instance, when we think of foods, such pairs of closely linked edibles that instantly come to mind include *meat and potatoes, peanut butter and jelly,* and, of course, *green eggs and ham.* Similarly, in the assessment arena, the most common pair of tag-team terms you'll encounter are *validity and* **reliability***.* In the preceding chapter, you saw that assessment validity is, by far, the most important concept in all of educational testing. Well, its close buddy, reliability, isn't all that far behind. Let's see why.

First off, a definition of "reliability" is surely in order. Happily, in one sense, a definition of assessment reliability is easy to identify. This is because—when considering reliability as it relates to educational testing—one synonym immediately comes to mind. It is *consistency.* Indeed, if you build all of your reliability-related thoughts atop the following equivalencies, you'll invariably be on solid ground:

Reliability = Consistency

Yes, assessment reliability refers to the consistency with which we measure whatever we are measuring. In education, of course, reliability usually signifies the consistency with which we measure people, typically *little* people. Moreover, assessment reliability is definitely a good thing, capable of inducing positive reactions like those stemming from the mention of motherhood, apple pie, or cuddly puppies. Assessment reliability, for those who mess around with educational tests, is an attribute to be cherished.

Nonetheless, assessment reliability comes to us accompanied by a handful of serious "wrinkles" that must be understood if we're going to get the most mileage out of educational tests. The most significant of these reliability wrinkles will be treated in this chapter. We can begin such wrinkle treating by first drawing one salient distinction between the concepts of assessment validity and assessment reliability.

RELIABILITY DWELLS IN TESTS

You will recall from Chapter 4's description of assessment validity that contrary to a widely held belief, validity does not reside in a test itself but, rather, is found in the accuracy of a score-based inference's contribution to a test's intended use. "Valid tests," you saw, do not exist. Instead, validity refers to the degree of accuracy with which a score-based inference supports a test's chief purpose. Thus, regarding validity, the focus is on the appropriateness of a particular test-based inference, not on the test itself.

For reliability, however, this game definitely changes. Assessment reliability resides in the test itself. Thus, we need to determine the degree to which a specific test measures *whatever it is measuring* with sufficient reliability, that is, with adequate consistency. As you will soon see, measurement specialists have—over the years—chosen several favorite indicators for describing the degree to which a test is reliable. Accordingly, we take a look at the most common of those indicators in this chapter.

It is worth mentioning that certain variables measured by educational tests are, by their very nature, less consistent than other variables. For example, a person's reading abilities often vary depending on the time of day when the reading is done, the nature of what's read, or the reader's perception regarding the importance of what's read. Indeed, the stability of many variables with which educators are concerned often vary. Such inconsistencies need to be recognized when interpreting estimates of a particular test's reliability, that is, how consistent was the thing being assessed?

Okay, so it is apparent that the fundamental nature of reliability seems sufficiently straightforward. Why is there any confusion, any at all, regarding assessment reliability? Well, one source of such confusion flows from the several ways in which members of the measurement community have, over the years, chosen to describe a test's reliability. Let's turn our attention now to those meaningfully different representations of reliability.

A Trio of Reliability Indicators

As you saw in the preceding chapter, when attempting to determine the validity of test-based inferences consonant with a test's primary purpose, measurement mavens try to collect *evidence* about the accuracy of score-based inferences, and also about the contribution that those score-based inferences make to the accomplishment of a test's primary purpose. In a similar manner, evidence regarding a particular test's consistency is collected to help us judge a test's reliability. In fact, three different kinds of reliability evidence are singled out in the joint AERA *Standards* (2014) as professionally sanctioned variations of reliability evidence. These three types of reliability evidence are *test-retest evidence, alternate-form evidence,* and *internal consistency evidence.* Sometimes thought of as different kinds of reliability, these three types of evidence represent distinctively different but important ways of determining an educational test's reliability. Let's look, briefly, at each of these three reliability indicators.

Test-retest reliability evidence. When a teacher administers an important test to students on, say, a Tuesday, the teacher typically assumes that if the same test had been administered one day later, on Wednesday, students' scores would be pretty much the same. Oh, not all scores, of course, would be perfectly identical. After all, Dazzling Dora, who typically aces all of this teacher's exams, might have been afflicted by the flu on Tuesday—hence would score poorly on the Tuesday test. But Dora, fully recovered, would have earned her typical superscore one day later. Similarly, several other students' rank-order positions on the two tests might have been somewhat different. Nevertheless, let's assume that most students' performances on the Tuesday and Wednesday tests were mighty similar. If the teacher were to compute a *correlation coefficient* between the students' Tuesday and Wednesday scores, the result is described as a *test-retest reliability coefficient.*

Without going into a lengthy explanation of how correlation coefficients are computed, it is sufficient for our purposes here to indicate that a correlation coefficient constitutes a numerical indication representing the strength and direction of a relationship between two variables. In this example, it's the relationship between the two sets of students' test scores, that is, students' scores on the Tuesday test and their scores on the same test, but taken on Wednesday. Correlation coefficients can range from a plus 1.00 to a minus 1.00, with high positive coefficients signifying that students' scores on one test were quite similar to their scores on the other test. Thus, a test-retest reliability coefficient of, say, .89 would indicate that students who were high scorers on the Tuesday test were usually high scorers on the Wednesday test. Similarly, based on a positive test-retest reliability coefficient of .89, students who did not score very well on the Tuesday test would also tend to be low-scorers on the Wednesday test. A correlation coefficient near zero would indicate that there was no meaningful relationship between students' performances on the two tests.

Test-retest reliability coefficients represent the *stability* with which a test is measuring what it is measuring. If an educational test is used at different times during a school year, whether the test is a teacher-made classroom quiz or a state's annual accountability exam, the greater the evidence of stability, the more confidence we can have in the decisions we intend to base, at least in part, on the test's results.

When test-retest reliability coefficients are computed, we need to pay attention to such factors as the length of delay between the two test administrations. Clearly, the longer the gap between the two testing sessions, the less likelihood that the two sets of scores will be similar. Some students will, during a lengthy between-testing gap, forget stuff. The longer the delay when collecting test-retest reliability evidence, the lower a resulting reliability coefficient is apt to be. It is also important—when hoping to secure a strongly positive test-retest correlation—to make sure that no significant instructional events have taken place between the two tests. If students received some serious instruction dealing with whatever is being measured by the test, then such instruction is almost certain to reduce the strength of any test-retest reliability coefficient.

In most instances involving a between-testing interval of a few days or so—with no test-related instruction having intervened—we often see test-retest reliability coefficients for classroom tests of between .70 and .80. Such correlations indicate that reasonable levels of stability exist for the test being studied. When reliability coefficients get much lower than, say, .70, most measurement specialist's get uneasy about assessment consistency. With few exceptions, reliability coefficients for commercially created standardized tests are much higher than those computed for teacher-made classroom tests. This is because, of course, commercially generated standardized tests toss all sorts of consistency-enhancing procedures at their emerging assessments.

Alternate-form reliability evidence. A second sort of reliability evidence deals with the degree to which *different forms* of a test yield results that are consistent. A number of real-world situations arise in our schools when different forms of a test— particularly different forms of a high-stakes standardized test—must be used for certain students. To illustrate, suppose a state's education authorities require high-school students to pass a test measuring a student's competence in reading, mathematics, composition, and science. If the state's students don't pass this four-part exam, then those unsuccessful students will not receive a state-approved high-school diploma. Clearly, this exam would be regarded as a high-stakes test by the test-takers—as well as by their families.

Well, what happens if certain students, for a host of legitimate reasons, including ill health or family emergencies, cannot take this diploma-denial test when it is initially administered? In fairness, officials of our fictitious state might have established a policy that allows such students additional opportunities to take the diploma-linked test. However, because subsequent administrations of the exam may consist of different forms of the initially administered test, then evidence is often assembled to demonstrate that the two alternate (supposedly equivalent) forms of the exam do, in fact, constitute an equally difficult challenge for test-takers.

In a manner not unlike what we saw for the collection of test-retest reliability evidence, what's done in the case of *alternate-form reliability evidence* is to require at least a sample of likely test-takers to complete two different forms of a test, then calculate a correlation coefficient based on their two sets of resultant scores. The result of such a correlation calculation, then, constitutes what's called an alternate-form reliability coefficient. In this instance, with the four subtests that constitute the diploma-denial exam, four separate alternate-form reliability coefficients would most likely be computed—one for each of the four subtests.

Often, if a relatively short period of time elapses between administrations of two alternate forms, and no instructionally significant events took place between the two test-administrations, we once more find alternate-form reliability coefficients for teacher-made tests hovering between .70 and .85. Given the greater care that typically goes into the creation of standardized achievement tests, alternate-form reliability indices for such tests often range between .75 and .90. Obviously, if alternate forms of a test are employed, the decisions riding on the test's results are more important and therefore stronger alternate-form consistency should be sought.

Internal consistency reliability evidence. When considering this final type of reliability evidence, please think back to the Chapter 2 description of the emergence of a comparison-focused view of educational testing that was fostered by the development of World War I's *Army Alpha.* The thrust of this testing was to identify Army recruits who would be good candidates for the U.S. Army's officer training programs. The *Alpha* was, in essence, a group-administered intelligence test. It sought to compare recruits according to their relative levels of smarts, and many of the architects of the test regarded what it was measuring to be a test-taker's *general intelligence* (sometimes referred to as *G-factor*).

Although we could surely determine the *Alpha's* test-retest reliability (by readministering the test) as well as its alternate-form reliability (because the test was provided in different forms), there was an altogether different kind of measurement "consistency" of interest to the *Alpha's* developers. This conception of consistency focused on the *consistency among the test's items* in what they were measuring. If, to illustrate, the idea behind this World War I test was to come up with comparative rankings among test-takers so that they could be contrasted with respect to their G-factor levels, then what the test's developers wanted was for all of a test form's items to measure essentially the same thing. Thus, the notion of *internal consistency reliability* had arrived, and its use has persisted—or, more accurately, its use has dominated—up to the present.

Internal consistency reliability is particularly important when a test is built so that all of its items are intended to measure the same thing. If a test attempts to measure discernbly different things, such as three truly distinguishable cognitive skills, then a really high internal consistency coefficient would suggest that the test's items appear to be measuring the same, unitary thing, not three separate things. What a test developer would *not* wish to see in such an instance would be a strong, positive internal consistency coefficient.

> Accordingly, if someone touting an educational test's reliability proudly trots out evidence to support that contention, make certain that such a stance is not based on the wrong reliability evidence.

As was the case with the two kinds of reliability evidence we considered earlier, internal consistency reliability coefficients can range from a plus 1.00 to a minus 1.00. This type of reliability evidence is provided far more frequently than its two reliability cousins. One reason for such an imbalance is that the computation of test-retest reliability and alternate-form reliability requires at least two test-administrations, whereas the computation of an internal consistency coefficient needs only one test-administration. For high-stakes standardized tests, because numerous item-development revisions can isolate items that appear to be functioning differently from the bulk of a test's items—so those atypical items can be revised or removed—internal consistency reliability coefficients are often strongly positive, for instance, .95 or so.

We are dealing with three considerably different, professionally approved (AERA, 2014) ways of thinking about a test's consistency. These three types of reliability evidence are most definitely *not* interchangeable. Accordingly, if someone touting an educational test's reliability proudly trots out evidence to support that contention, make certain that such a stance is not based on the wrong reliability evidence.

Sadly, such blatantly off-target support for a test's reliability is much more common than you'd think. In the most common misapplication of reliability estimates for educational tests, test developers tend to compute internal consistency reliability estimates and describe them as "the test's reliability," even though, for the test's intended use, the homogeneity of the test's items may be of scant practical interest.

Wrap-Up Reliability Wrinkles

Earlier in the chapter, I indicated that although reliance on a test's reliability meshes well with a common-sense approach to educational testing, there are several reliability wrinkles that must be addressed. You've just seen one really important wrinkle dealing with the three distinctively dissimilar forms of reliability evidence. The other two wrinkles you should be alerted to deal with are (1) the use of *decision-consistency estimates* versus reliance on more widely used correlation-based reliability coefficients such as a test-retest reliability coefficient and (2) whether we're focusing on assessment consistency for *groups* versus looking at assessment consistency for *individual* test-takers.

Decision-consistency estimates. For more than a century, those engaged in U.S. educational testing have almost always reported a test's reliability as a correlation-based reliability coefficient. More often than not, as noted above, the particular reliability indicator involved has been an internal consistency coefficient.

But we often use educational tests in order to arrive at particular *decisions* about the students who complete those tests. And it is for this reason that an increasingly popular way of characterizing a test's reliability has surfaced in recent years. These representations of reliability are labeled *decision-consistency estimates,* and their name pretty well indicates how they function. Their focus is not on the consistency of a student's test *score* but, rather, on the consistency of the *decision* that's based on a student's score. An illustration should help clarify how a decision-consistency approach works.

Let's assume a school district's school board has reached a policy decision: If the eighth-grade students do not pass a brand new "Mathematical Fundamentals Exam," those students will be required to take a separate remedial math course in the ninth grade. A passing score of 75 points (out of 100 points) has been set for the new math exam. And two alternate—but supposedly parallel—forms of the test have been developed. In an effort to determine the reliability (alternate-form reliability) of the new test, about ninety eighth-grade students in a nearby district agreed to take both forms of the new math exam on two consecutive days. The results are seen in Figure 5.1—along with a bold-face index of decision consistency for the two forms:

Figure 5.1   An Example of How to Calculate
Decision-Consistency

Students Passing (Scoring 75 or Above) Both Times = 62%
Students Failing (Scoring 74 or Below) Both Times = 27%
Students Passing Then Failing, or Failing Then Passing = 11%
Decision-Consistency Index = 89%

Decision-consistency indices, as you can see, are based only on the *decisions* resulting from students' test performance. Such indicators of reliability are not particularly concerned about the relative similarity of test-takers' *scores.* So, for example, if Maria had earned a score of 96 when she first took the new math fundamentals test, but dropped down to a 76 when she once again took the test, it makes no difference for purposes of this indicator of reliability. She passed both times. Decision-consistency estimates, such as the 89 percent seen above, are based on the proportion of test-takers whose scores resulted in identical decisions (the 62 percent and the 27 percent in this example).

Because most people can derive intuitive meaning more readily from percentages than from correlation coefficients, many measurement specialists are beginning to rely on decision-consistency estimates when they report reliability results—often in addition to the more traditional display of correlation-based reliability coefficients.

> The kinds of reliability coefficients usually reported for educational tests provide us with estimates of consistency for groups of students, not for individual students.

The standard error of measurement. Thus far in the chapter we have been considering reliability, and the three forms of evidence typically used to represent it, in relation to the measurement consistency of *groups* of test-takers. To illustrate, when we collect evidence that there's a strong, positive test-retest reliability for a particular test—such as is seen in a test-retest coefficient of .88—then we can safely conclude that if a group of students were to retake the same test that they've already taken, their relative performances on the second test will wind up pretty similar to their relative performances on the first test. The kinds of reliability coefficients usually reported for educational tests provide us with estimates of consistency for groups of students, not for individual students.

Happily, there's also an indicator of consistency that can be used when focusing on the consistency of an individual student's performance, and it's called the **standard error of measurement.** A standard error of measurement (SEM) functions much like the plus-or-minus error bands we often see accompanying sample-based opinion surveys. Along with the reported results, we usually see plus-or-minus error margins in an SEM that can be used to estimate just how consistent the reported scores actually are. To illustrate, if Christopher answered fifty items correctly on an educational test of seventy items, we could use this particular test's SEM of, say, 5 points to estimate that if Christopher were once more to take the same test, he would have correctly answered between forty-five and fifty-five items about two-thirds of the time. That is, he would have earned a score of 50 plus or minus 1 SEM (in this example consisting of 5 points).

If the score-reports that parents receive for their in-school children do a decent job of describing how an SEM works, most parents find SEMs helpful when attempting to make sense out of their children's scores on standardized tests. Teachers, of course, rarely have the time or energy to generate standard errors of measurement for their own classroom exams. Nonetheless, such SEMs could be computed, and they would accurately signify that educational tests—whether teacher-made or standardized exams—are far from unerringly accurate. The inferences that can be drawn from educational tests are useful, but typically much less precise than most people imagine.

By using the reliability coefficient chosen for a particular test, and by incorporating an indication of the degree of *score-spread* among test-takers (typically signified by a score distribution's **standard deviation** reflecting the variability among a set of scores), it is possible to calculate an SEM that can be used when making a test-based decision about a particular student.

Takeaway Time

Although the central meaning of assessment reliability is readily graspable as a reflection of the consistency with which a test is measuring whatever it's measuring, a satisfactory understanding of reliability hinges also on one's understanding of several reliability nuances associated with this important measurement concept. The most important of these are collapsed in the chapter understanding seen below.

Assessment Reliability. *Assessment reliability, the consistency with which an educational test measures what it's measuring, is indicated by three conceptually different kinds of evidence and can be calculated either for test-taker groups or for individual test-takers.*

As always, when considering a test's reliability, and as you saw early in the chapter, reliability is a test-specific attribute. So, please rely mostly on common sense. The more important the stakes associated with a test's use, the more important it is to demonstrate that a test is sufficiently reliable. It is especially important, however, to match the type of reliability evidence supplied with the specific purpose for which an educational test is used. For example, if two different forms of a test are used as a diploma-denial exam for high-school students, then an alternate-form indicator of reliability should clearly be used rather than either of the other two types of reliability indicators.

Elsewhere (Popham, 2017), I have recommended that because of the hassle involved in calculating the correct kind of reliability data, classroom teachers should secure reliability evidence for only a very small number of their most important teacher-made tests—if any at all. For all high-stakes standardized tests, however, the provision of *purpose-compatible* reliability evidence is mandatory.

6

Fairness in Testing

A Long Time Coming

When testing children, as in all realms of human endeavor, fairness is laudable—unfairness is lamentable. We praise what is fair, we deride its opposite. Interestingly, in educational testing it was not always thus.

Although today's architects of educational tests, especially the architects of high-stakes educational tests, understand all too well the perils of creating an unfair test, the architects of yesteryear's educational tests were—with precious few exceptions—essentially unaware of the fairness with which their tests were measuring students' abilities. I know this sounds implausible—particularly when we are so often reminded these days of the lack of fairness in many education areas—but if you turn back the time clock about three decades, you'll find that fairness in educational testing during that era received almost zero attention. How come?

HIGH-STAKES TRIGGER EQUITY CONCERNS

In previous chapters, you learned that we have been using educational tests in this nation for more than a century. Well, if you were to take a serious dive into history—for instance, if you headed back to see what was going on during the *first* half of America's educational-testing century—you'd rarely, if ever, find anyone writing about—or even thinking about—the fairness with which educators were testing their students.

Such inattention to the fairness of educational testing did not occur because educational testers were fundamentally unfair folks. No, even back then, if you were explicitly to ask a sizeable group of individuals involved in the building of standardized tests whether educational tests should be fair or unfair, you'd surely get nothing but an a capella chorus of pro-fairness responses. During the early days of educational testing in the United States, however, few of those same fair-minded individuals ever gave any *serious* consideration to the fairness of their tests.

Almost all of the attention of the early builders of educational assessments was centered on coming up with devices that would do an *accurate* job of measurement, that is, an accurate testing of the aptitude or achievement of the students being assessed. During the first few decades of educational testing, those who were creating such tests were, clearly, shaping and sharpening their craft. They were discovering how best to elicit students' item-by-item responses so that a student's total test scores would lead to an accurate inference about the student. Improving the precision of educational testing was, of course, a reasonable focus in the early days of such testing.

However, "way back then" we rarely made any genuinely significant decisions based on students' test performances. Test results were provided to educators, but in general it was up to educators to determine whether any serious action was to take place because of students' test performances. Educational tests, up until the enactment of the *Elementary and*

Secondary Education Act (ESEA) of 1965—roughly a half-century ago—were typically "low stakes" or even "no stakes" measurement instruments. But as you are now well aware, ESEA began to change the testing landscape because decisions regarding future federal funding of state and district programs began being linked to the quality of students' test performances.

Even though we saw the results of educational tests being used for increasingly higher-stakes decisions, such subtle shifts failed to dramatically increase attention to test fairness. Indeed, substantially increased attention to test fairness did not arrive until certain states began denying high-school diplomas to those students who could not pass a state-required competency test, one that measured students' mastery of rudimentary skills and knowledge, typically in reading, writing, and mathematics. At that point we saw widespread denials of diplomas to high-school students who, until the installation of such a test-passage requirement, would most likely have received their high-school diplomas. Serious high-stakes testing had most definitely sauntered on stage in America.

> It became apparent that, along with validity and reliability, test fairness had become the bona fide third member of educational testing's "blessed trinity."

We soon discovered that meaningfully greater numbers of minority students, especially African-American students, were being denied diplomas than were their white classmates. What was going on? Based on such disparities in diploma denials, could we conclude that African-American children had received a lower quality education? Or was it, perhaps, that the tests being used were biased against African-American children? In the ensuing years, those who were developing any sort of high-stakes educational test, whether linked to a decision such as diploma-denial or to the more general overall evaluation of schools, began to refine the procedures they were using to increase the fairness of their educational tests. In this chapter you will be considering several procedures, seriously studied during recent years, that are now regarded as capable of reducing the unfairness of educational testing.

A BOOST FROM THE JOINT STANDARDS

Earlier, in Chapter 2, you learned that the American Educational Research Association (AERA) *Standards for Educational and Psychological Testing* (2014) exert considerable influence on what takes place in this nation regarding educational testing. Such influence stems chiefly from reliance by many judges on the joint *Standards* when engaged in test-related courtroom litigation. Accordingly, when members of the measurement community saw that the July 2014 edition of the joint *Standards* contains a brand new chapter focusing exclusively on educational fairness, it became apparent that, along with validity and reliability, test fairness had become the bona fide third member of educational testing's "blessed trinity."

A description of its overarching *fairness standard* captures the thrust of the joint *Standards'* insistence on fairness:

> All steps in the testing process, including test design, validation, development, administration and scoring procedures, should be designed in such a manner as to minimize construct-irrelevant variance and to promote valid score interpretations for the intended uses for all examinees in the intended population. (AERA *Standards*, 2014, p. 63)

Most of the language in this standard is readily understandable except for the phrase, *"construct-irrelevant variance."* What this label refers to is any factor in test-takers' scores that, attributable to extraneous factors, might distort the meaning of those scores. For instance, if several "story-problem" items on a mathematics test relied on sports-related contexts apt to be more familiar to boys than girls, then some girls' scores might be lower than they actually should be—simply because those girls didn't know about baseball's "infield fly rule" or football's "fair catch" rule. Thus, a student's gender would become a construct-irrelevant variable in such an instance. Similarly, if a student's performance is dependent on test-takers' socioeconomic status or on familiarity with certain religious concepts, those extraneous factors might often distort a student's score. Such distortions, of course, would reduce the accuracy of interpretations based on test-takers' scores. The reason we attempt to enhance fairness in educational testing is because—if we didn't—then construct-irrelevant variance would diminish the validity of our score-based inferences for intended test-score uses.

The 2014 joint *Standards,* as in previous versions of that document, emphasizes *assessment bias* as a central threat to fairness in educational testing. We will look at such bias soon—and how to minimize it. However, two relatively new concepts are singled out in the joint *Standards* that warrant special consideration.

The first of these is *accessibility,* and it refers to the notion that all test-takers should be provided with an unobstructed opportunity to demonstrate their status regarding what is being measured without being impeded by factors irrelevant to whatever is being assessed. If students who are currently learning English, for example, are asked to display certain mathematical skills by using English-laden test items that they do not understand, then this will surely distort those students' performances on the math test.

> The joint *Standards* stress the importance of focusing on fairness at every step in the assessment of students, that is, from the initial building of a test all the way through its evaluation, administration, scoring, and interpretation.

Another procedure advocated in the joint *Standards* is *universal design,* an approach to test-design that—from the very earliest moments when constructing an educational test—strives to maximize accessibility to the test for all students. By making all test-design decisions from the very get-go so that those decisions enhance accessibility, the resultant tests are apt to be more accessible to all students, hence more fair.

One other fairness-related procedure should be kept in mind by those involved in educational testing. The joint *Standards* stress the importance of focusing on fairness at every step in the assessment of students, that is, from the initial building of a test all the way through its evaluation, administration, scoring, and interpretation.

Well, along the way, we often find that we must employ suitable forms of **accommodation**. Accommodations are adjustments made at any point in the assessment process that do not alter the fundamental nature of the content being assessed. For example, if a test of students' reading skill were being presented to a visually impaired student, the use of an extra-large font for a test's items would be an appropriate accommodation. If, however, the items on a reading-skills test were to be read aloud to a visually impaired student, this would constitute an essential change in the nature of the "reading" skill being measured. The function of assessment accommodations is to increase the fairness with which certain students are being assessed, yet not alter the essence of what's being assessed. This is, as you might guess, easier to advocate than to accomplish.

ASSESSMENT BIAS AND ITS REDUCTION

Assessment bias refers to qualities of an assessment instrument that offend or unfairly penalize a group of students because of students' gender, race, ethnicity, socioeconomic status, religion, or other group-defining characteristics. Although full-blown fairness in educational testing calls for attention to equity at every phase of the assessment process, not just during the scrutiny of under-development test items, much attention in recent years has centered on the diminishment of bias in the items that make up an educational test. Based on substantial activity in this arena, two prominent procedures for reducing assessment bias are now regarded as acceptable. We will briefly consider both.

Judgmental reviews. Asking a group of individuals to function as a **bias-review** panel for evaluating the items intended for use in a test has become, these days, almost a requirement for those developing any kind of high-stakes educational test. Here's how such reviews work. A carefully chosen group of individuals—for example, adults who are representative of those minority students who will ultimately be completing an exam—are asked to review, one-by-one, the items that, if approved, will constitute a particular examination. The twenty to thirty or so members of the bias-review committee are often, but not necessarily, teachers. After a suitable orientation regarding the nature of assessment bias, the reviewers are then asked to register a judgment—for every item in the pool of potentially usable items—by supplying a Yes or No response to a question such as the following:

An Illustrative Per-Item Question for Bias Reviewers

Might this item offend or unfairly penalize any group of students on the basis of personal characteristics, such as gender, ethnicity, religion, or race?

Items identified by this judgmental process as being potentially biased are either edited—to make them less so—or discarded altogether.

Please note in the illustrative bias-review question for reviewers that the specific wording employed in such charges to reviewers can make gobs of difference in how bias reviewers regard an item. The illustrative question seen here asks "*Might* this item offend . . . ?" This phrasing will elicit more identifications of potentially biased items than would a phrasing such as "*Will* this item offend . . . ?" In short, the "Might" question turns out to be a more stringent bias-detection question than its "Will" counterpart. That's because the "Might" version is almost certain to detect more potentially biased items than is the higher demand "Will" question. To really understand whether the bias review of a test's items has been suitably rigorous, one needs to examine the actual language employed with item reviewers, which can vary enormously.

Empirical scrutiny. Whereas a bias-review panel functions *prior* to an actual tryout of test items with real test-takers, once the items on a test are available for actual field-testing, then those items are usually field-tested to carry out what is called a **differential item functioning** (DIF) analysis. A substantial number of students is required to carry out a DIF analysis, with the more students involved, the better. Here's how it works.

First off, the student groups involved are identified, for instance, Hispanic-American students, African-American students, and white students. Then the items to field-test are administered to the entire pool of students. For every item, performance levels are computed for each of the identified groups of test-takers in an attempt to identify any items that are functioning differently for the student-groups involved. If, for example, we discover on a particular item (let's say it was *Item 34*) that although 76 percent of the white students answered the item correctly, only 39 percent of the Hispanic-Americans answered it correctly, and only 44 percent of the African-American students came up with a correct answer. Such an item might be one in which a student's getting a correct answer is dependent on the student's familiarity with the way that passports are used during international travel. In the school district where the passport-related item was used, however, most white students' families are decisively more affluent than Hispanic-American and African-American families, so white students have taken part in many more passport-requisite trips than their less affluent class-mates. A "passport conversance" item such as seen below where Choice C is the correct answer, therefore, beclouds the true achievement levels of the African-American and Hispanic-American test-takers.

Item 34. Which one of the following statements most accurately captures the way American travelers use their official passports when entering most foreign nations?

  A. A U.S. passport must be surrendered upon entering a foreign country to a passport-control agency at the border, to be reclaimed when leaving that country.

  B. Only U.S. citizens who have been convicted of a felony are obliged to surrender their passports at the border of a foreign nation.

  C. American travelers, in most instances, must display an official, governmentally issued passport to enter a foreign nation, but then retain their passports.

  D. In most cases, U.S. citizens who do not possess an official passport must sign a formal "Non-Passport Promissory" agreement when entering almost every foreign country.

Incidentally, a group of students' average percent-correct on an item is usually signified as that item's *p-value*. Thus, an item with an overall *p*-value of .63 would have been answered correctly by 63 percent of all the test-takers. Well, given the average *p*-value disparities between white students and the other two groups of students, *Item 34* would be seriously reviewed in an effort to determine if any shortcomings seem to exist—that is, any biased elements in the item that might have eluded the earlier scrutiny of a bias-review group. If weaknesses are present in the item, it would then be edited or jettisoned. Although DIF analyses are usually carried out using more sophisticated statistical indicators than item p-values, such analyses are structurally similar to the procedural essentials just described.

It is important to note that disparities in the difficulties of items do *not* automatically reveal the presence of item bias. What may be detected by disparities in DIF analyses might, instead, represent weak instruction previously provided to particular subgroups of students. It may not be the test itself that is biased but, rather, a bias in the caliber of certain students' prior instruction.

Although much of this chapter's focus has been on the diminishment of unfairness in high-stakes standardized tests, and particularly the isolation of items that suffer from assessment bias, unfairness can also be present in teacher-made classroom tests. Clearly, most busy teachers do not have the time or resources to enlist the support of an external item-review group, nor do teachers typically have access to enough students to carry out DIF analyses on their tests' items. However, if classroom teachers are sensitized to the possibility of unfairness in their tests, and attend to equity considerations from the original building of a classroom assessment until it has been administered, scored, and interpreted, odds are that a teacher's classroom tests will definitely be less biased. For example, a teacher whose students include many Latino children might ask one of her colleagues to look over a test's items to see if there are any elements in the items that might offend or unfairly penalize a Hispanic student. This is far less elaborate than relying on the item-by-item judgments of a panel of reviewers, but it is surely better than nothing at all. If teachers try to be extra attentive to the issue of assessment bias as they crank out their own classroom tests, odds are that the resultant tests will be fairer.

Takeaway Time

Only in recent decades have members of the educational measurement community reached agreement on what constitutes fairness in educational testing. Such fairness is now seen as embracing the entire educational-assessment process, starting with the very beginning of test development and extending through every significant phase of assessment usage all the way until students' scores contribute to test-based decisions. A significant along-the-way step helping to ensure such fairness calls for the reduction of item bias by the use of both judgmental and, when possible, empirical procedures.

Fairness in Testing. *Fairness in educational testing, now seen to be as important as validity and reliability in the construction and evaluation of tests, must be carefully documented–employing both judgmental and empirical procedures–to maximally minimize assessment bias.*

With respect to the nature of unfairness in assessment, you have seen that we now devote much more attention to the eradication of unfair testing, and that both judgmental and empirical procedures should be used whenever possible. If you are interested in learning more about the fairness-enhancing procedures employed with any particular educational test, this is another instance where any group with which you are affiliated may wish to enlist the services of an assessment specialist who can provide an appraisal of the rigor—and zeal—with which fairness has been sought for a particular test. The judgmental item reviews employed for this purpose are really quite straightforward, as is the logic involved in empirical analyses of item bias. The quest for assessment fairness is based, as is true with all aspects of educational testing, on simple good sense.

7

Reporting Results

Where Rubber and Road Meet

As has often been mentioned during our six-chapter gallop through Assessment Land, the underlying reason that teachers test students is to arrive at score-based inferences about those students' covert knowledge and skills. When informed by such inferences, teachers can then make more defensible decisions about how to instruct their students. In a similar manner, once parents of school-age children acquire a reasonably accurate idea of their children's academic strengths and weaknesses, those parents can then provide at-home activities for children to help remedy weaknesses and build on strengths. By relying on test-based inferences about students' abilities, both educators and parents are more apt to arrive at appropriate next-step actions. Deriving inferences about students' unseen skills and knowledge based on their test scores, quite clearly, makes much more sense than simply guessing.

But after students have completed a test, how do their scores become transported to educators and parents? Well, if we're talking about a standardized test, in almost every instance we learn about a student's test performance by relying on a *score report*. Indeed, for any sort of large-scale educational test, it is impossible to arrive at score-based inferences about particular students without access to score reports for those students. In this chapter, we'll take a brief look at today's score reports and what to focus on when using such reports.

As you will soon see, it is a student's score report that allows an educator—or a parent—to identify what a student's test scores actually are and, having done so, to then rely on those scores to arrive at an inference regarding what it is that a student knows and can do. Please note that when we start arriving at score-based inferences derived from a particular test, it is imperative to make sure the primary *purpose* for which that particular educational test has been developed *coincides directly* with the score-based inferences we're attempting to make. The confidence that can be placed in any score-based inference depends directly on the way in which an educational test has been constructed. When a test is created for a purpose that meshes with the score-based inferences being drawn, then all is at peace in the Halls of Measurement Heaven.

Reports for Standardized Tests: Increasingly Important, Increasingly Opaque

In general, when teacher-created *classroom* tests are used, the scoring procedures employed are relatively straightforward. Such scoring procedures (for instance, "Number of Items Answered Correctly") are readily understandable. Moreover, teachers are quite knowledgeable about how they're intending to use the results from their classroom tests and the kinds of score-based inferences they intend to make about their students. Because the results of classroom tests are typically reportable in fairly simple ways, not much confusion surrounds the reporting of students' performances for almost all classroom tests. Such is not the case with regard to externally developed and formally administered standardized tests.

With such standardized tests, the way that score reports are structured often results in profound user-intimidation. We'll now take a quick look at how to interpret standardized tests' reports accurately. And, of course, the clarity and ease of making sense out of standardized tests' reports will always hinge on the particulars of a specific score report. Some reports are readily decipherable. Other reports seem to have been devised by sadists relying on cryptography.

It is occasionally useful to realize how the arrival of electronic scoring procedures has sometimes caused score reporting to be regarded as an inscrutable enterprise hidden behind opaque curtains. Let's face it, about a half-century ago, performances on standardized tests were scored by in-person human beings—one item at a time. Early score reports typically ended up with the identification of a test-taker's "number correct." But then, after years of such "hand scoring," we saw the arrival of electronically scoreable response sheets that permitted scoring machines to instantly scan students' responses to flocks of multiple-choice items. Following such a spate of scanned-sheet scoring, we then saw increasingly sophisticated computers automatically score students' responses to selected-response items, and even to score students' responses to short-answer items. Surely within the next few years, we'll witness the routine scoring of students' lengthier essay responses by scoring protocols relying on artificial-intelligence digital devices.

Moreover, even the forms of tests that students are obliged to complete these days are becoming more sophisticated. To illustrate, *computer-based testing* has now been with us for a good many years. In computer-based testing, students not only receive a test's items via a computer (or by means of some comparable device, such as an electronic tablet or a smartphone), but students also submit their responses via computers. In such instances, a computer serves as little more than a relay device between the assessed and the assessor.

Even more impressive, in recent years we have seen the increasingly widespread use of *computer-adaptive testing* in which, based on a student's success in responding to earlier computer-presented items, the student is given subsequent items more closely matched to the student's by-then-estimated ability level. Such individualized computer-abetted dispensations of items, because the later items presented to a student are much closer to the student's ability level, can save substantial test-taking time in determining a student's ability level. For computer-adaptive testing, as you can see, test-takers often receive substantially different sets of items from the sets of items presented to other test-takers. Score reports capable of coherently describing a student's perfor-mances in the midst of these sorts of complexities are most definitely not "your grandfather's score reports."

Score-Reporting Procedures

Before turning to a description of the most common ways that score reports usually describe students' performances on standardized tests, two issues need to be stressed. The first of these stems from the purpose for which an educational test is used.

As was emphasized in Chapter 2, the three measurement missions of educational tests are *comparative, instructional,* and *evaluative.* Score reports should provide guidance for making inferences that are in accord with a test's primary pur-pose. For instance, if a standardized test portrays itself as a *diagnostic test*, that is, as an assessment intended to isolate a student's strengths and weaknesses, then the test must

> The clarity of score reporting lies with the score reporter, not with the user of a score report. Those who use score reports should always demand nothing less than score-reporting lucidity.

include enough items so that valid inferences can be made about the different instructional "sub-targets" being measured. Without such diagnostic pinpointing, it is essentially impossible to defend a supposedly "diagnostic" test's reports as being *instructionally* useful.

A second emphasis when working with students' score reports is that it is the responsibility of those who fashion a score report to make it *comprehensible* to those using the report. That's right, those who design a score report must present the report in an intuitively interpretable fashion. The clarity of score reporting lies with the score reporter, not with the user of a score report. Those who use score reports should always demand nothing less than score-reporting lucidity, for instance, by submitting a written complaint, digitally or on real paper, about the clarity of a score report. Teachers and school administrators can complain to a district's leaders who, in turn, can register dissatisfaction with the agency or measurement firm dispensing the score reports. Parents, often cowed by the off-putting nature of their children's score reports, can let educators at their school know about the problem. Do not underestimate the potential of a few well-written cries for clarity in score reports. Parental complaints about score-report clarity have triggered dramatic changes in such reports during recent years in a good many school districts.

Remembering that we are focusing now on the most common score-reporting procedures for externally administered tests—typically standardized ones—let's consider the techniques frequently used by score-reporters to describe test-takers' performances. In turn, we'll briefly consider *percentiles, performance-level categories,* and *scale scores.*

Percentiles. Perhaps the most readily understood way of describing a student's performance on a high-stakes standardized test is to report the student's score as a percentile. As many people know, a percentile indicates the percent of test-takers whom a specific student's score exceeded. So, to illustrate, if a student's score on a state's annually administered accountability test had been reported at, say, the 79th percentile, then we could conclude that this student's score equaled or exceeded the scores of 79 percent of the students in whatever group of students was constituting the test's "norm group."

Often, for nationally standardized tests, such norm groups are represented by the performances of a carefully chosen, representative national sample of students who completed the same test soon after a particular test began being widely used. When a test is given only to students in a particular state, for instance, such as when a state's annual accountability tests are administered at particular grade levels in that state, the percentiles seen in score reports are usually based on all of the state's students who took the same test. Almost all standardized tests are accompanied by a technical manual, usually obtainable from the test-developer's website, describing key details of the norm group that was used for test-score interpretations.

Because of the way percentiles are calculated, they cannot be easily averaged so that a teacher could, for instance, compute a meaningful average percentile for an entire class. When using percentiles to interpret students' test scores, it is important that the "norm group" is up-to-date and representative of the students whose scores are being reported.

Performance-level categories. Another common way of representing a student's performance on an important test is to indicate in which of several *performance-level categories* a student's score falls. Often, such performance levels are similar to the categories suggested by federal lawmakers in, for instance, the *No Child Left Behind Act*, namely, *advanced, proficient, basic,* and *below basic.* Those categories, now widely used, are based on reporting categories first used when performances were reported for the **National Assessment of Educational Progress** (NAEP), an examination that for roughly a half-century has been measuring American students' mastery of important subjects at selected grade levels. When relying on the use of such performance-level categories, an attempt is made to set forth a continuum of low-to-high classifications of quality. It is important to know, however, how these categories have been created for use in reporting students' performances on a particular test and, quite often, in a particular setting (such as in the state where the test was administered).

Almost without exception, those in charge of reporting the results from a high-stakes test rely on some sort of *standard-setting study*. During such studies, a group of carefully selected, content-knowledgeable individuals initially review a test's actual items and the results of tryout data indicative of students' likely performances, then establish *cut-scores* to use when separating students into different performance categories. Thus, for example, it might be determined that students must reach a cut-score of at least 76 percent correct on a test to be assigned to the *proficient* category, but that a cut-score of at least 88 percent correct must be earned in order for a student to be identified at the next higher level—*advanced.*

> Given the significance of cut-scores for the designation of performance-level categories, any contributing standard-setting studies should be above reproach.

Because such judgmentally based standard-setting studies are so pivotal in the use of score reports based on performance-level categories, those using such reports should verify that the procedures employed during a particular test's standard-setting studies were both well conceived and properly implemented. Clearly, a shabbily conducted standard-setting study will lead to a reliance on less than defensible performance-level categories. It should not be assumed that the selection of the cut-scores for a really high-stakes test was automatically satisfactory. Given the significance of cut-scores for the designation of performance-level categories, any contributing standard-setting studies should be above reproach.

Scale scores. For a variety of statistical reasons, the most prevalent score-reporting systems used these days rely on *scale scores.* Users of reports featuring scale scores, therefore, should possess at least a general notion of how the number on those scales were spawned—and why. However, please don't get your expectations up too high regarding whether you'll be able to intuitively understand the meaning of many scale-score reports. You see, without some really helpful interpretive guidance from those who create a test's score report, the score-report user is frequently unable to make serious sense out of certain reports based on scale-scores.

When students have completed an educational test, they typically end up by earning some sort of *raw score,* that is, the number of score points they earned based on the number of items they answered properly. Sometimes a raw score is nothing more than the sum of how many items were answered correctly. For other tests, the isolation of a raw score is more complicated because certain items have been assigned different scoring weights. And sometimes, when computer adaptive tests are involved—whereby different students are asked to complete very different sets of items—the calculation of a student's raw score is consummately complicated.

But let's get fundamental for a moment. What's going on when scale scores are birthed is that a student's raw score on a test has been *statistically* converted to a new score that resides (happily, one hopes) on a brand new scale. Not wishing to assault you with an array of statistically compelling reasons for generating such new scales, please be assured that the numbers in an *arbitrarily chosen* new scale can range all over the lot, for example, from 100 to 300, from 10 to 60, or from 900 to 1,500 (depending on the scale-maker's preference). The resulting scale score, however, constitutes a sound statistical way of transforming test-takers' raw scores into a mathematically more meaningful set of new scores.

Sometimes, for example, the developers of an educational test wish to create a mean score of 100 on a 50-item test that, when used with many tryout students, has an actual arithmetic mean of 32. What's done, then, is to subtract 32 from 100 to arrive at a scale-score constant (in this example, 68) that when added to all scores transforms the original distribution of raw scores (with a mean of 32) to a new, spiffy scale-score distribution with a mean of 100. Nothing to it.

An illustration of how test-takers' raw scores are turned into scale scores is presented in Figure 7.1. You can see that the raw scores from a test (presented as the top line in the figure) range from zero to 40. These raw scores have been converted into scale scores (seen as the figure's lower line) ranging from 400 to 800 points. Figure 7.1's new 400 to 800 scale is, as noted earlier, quite arbitrary.

As you can then see in Figure 7.2, a student who ends up with a raw score of 30 points is then assigned a scale score of 700. What may not be apparent when you look at Figures 7.1 and 7.2 is that a scale score of 700 points, for teachers, parents, policymakers, and almost anyone else—*is quite meaningless.* That is, our imaginary student's 700 scale score really conveys no notion of worthiness or unworthiness to someone who's trying to snare some understandable meaning from a score report relying on scale scores. Most people can make sense out of percentiles because, over the years, we have formed impressions of what it means to score at high percentiles, middle percentiles, and low percentiles. But we have no experience whatsoever in drawing meaning

Figure 7.1   A Raw-Score Scale and a Converted-Score Scale

Raw-Score Scale	0	10	20	30	40
Scale Score	400	500	600	700	800

Figure 7.2   An Illustration of a Raw-Score's Conversion
to a Scale Score

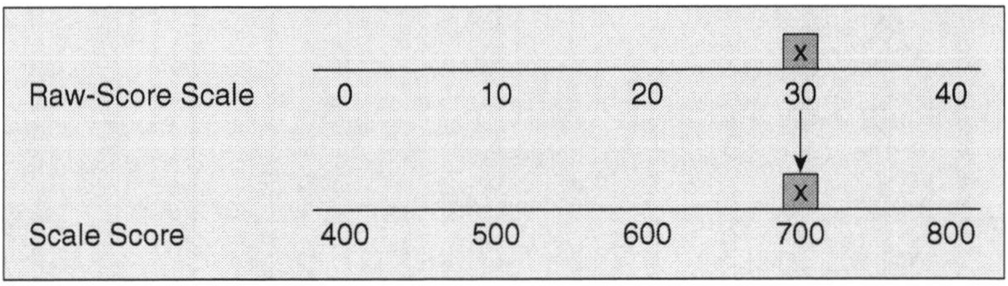

				x	
Raw-Score Scale	0	10	20	30	40
				↓	
				x	
Scale Score	400	500	600	700	800

from a 400- to 800-point scale—or from any similar arbitrarily created scale.

This is where the users of score reports dare not placidly accept what are sometimes fundamentally uninterpretable score reports. If a score report's scale scores are accompanied by at least some interpretation-support guidance, then the users of that scale-score–based reporting system might be able to make more *actionable* sense out of the scores presented. Of course, after a test has been used for several years and its scale scores have been reported for a few years, then users of the test's score reports will slowly begin to form at least some approximate ideas about what levels of scale scores constitute acceptable, stellar, or wretched performances. But "several years" may be too long to wait, at least for the students whose performances are reported during those several years. Often, if scale-score reports include at least rough approximations regarding the percent of students who typically earn particular scale-score levels, this information will satisfy most of those who must interpret such reports.

Teachers, parents, or policymakers who wish to take reasonable action based on students' scale-score reports should *demand* that the sometimes uninterpretable score reports accompanying many of today's standardized tests be buttressed by at least some interpretation guidance. Although today's scale-score reporting procedures may provide users with scads of statistical niceties, if those procedures sacrifice interpretive clarity, such a price is too high.

TAKEAWAY TIME

Test-based inferences about the students who complete most of today's high-stakes educational tests almost always arise from the score reports associated with those tests. Accordingly, it makes sense for those who wish to make truly defensible inferences about students to become conversant with the fundamentals of today's score reports. This abbreviated chapter, without reliance on serious statistical cavorting to draw meaning from such score reports, has attempted to underscore the chapter's chief takeaway.

> **Score-Reporting Rudiments.** *Because test-based inferences about student groups, or about individual students, are typically formulated from score reports, users of such reports should demand that the scores being reported are both easily interpretable and have been elicited by a test whose purpose coincides with those inferences.*

This chapter's chief understanding stresses a need for score reports to be easily understandable. Such clarity in score reporting typically requires score reports to embody a truly actionable *grain-size*, that is, a way of reporting students' performances at a level that's not too broad or too tiny but, Goldilocks-like, "just right" for test-based actions.

8

Formative Assessment

Instructional Magic?

One of the frequently stressed themes of this book's dip into educational testing is that such testing should not be seen as intimidating or complicated. On the contrary, as has often been reiterated, educational testing is, in essence, a set of commonsense procedures focused on figuring out what's going on inside students' skulls. Putting it differently, educational measurement's mission is to help us make accurate, actionable inferences about students' unseen knowledge and skills.

Well, this chapter on *formative assessment* attempts to drive that point home with zeal. What you'll be reading about is a marvelous *instructional* strategy that happens to be rooted in classroom *assessment.* It's an assessment-based teaching strategy that, after its bells and whistles have been stripped away, is nothing more complicated than the application of *ends-means* thinking to instruction.

ENDS-MEANS THINKING

No records exist to help us discern when ends-means thinking first flourished on earth, but we can safely wager it was many centuries ago. Back then, if prehistoric humans had a particular end in mind, such as trapping a marauding sabre-toothed tiger, they'd decide on a means to achieve the desired outcome— such as digging a deep pit—then see if the selected means actually worked. If the chosen means turned out to accomplish the desired end—in this example, a trapped tiger—then such a result would indicate that the selected means had been appropriately chosen. However, if the selected means proved to be unsuccessful—as evidenced by a still-on-the-loose sabre tooth—then those early tiger-trappers would frantically try out an adjusted approach such as digging a much deeper pit. The essence of ends-means thinking, of course, is that if a chosen approach to the accomplishment of a goal does not work, then a different approach is selected. As a goal-achievement strategy, ends-means thinking, through the centuries, has proven its worth. It is a winning way of dealing with the world.

Well, ends-means thinking is precisely what goes on when teachers employ formative assessment in their own classrooms. As you'll see in this chapter, formative assessment works—and it works remarkably well. However, because formative assessment is simply an educational application of ends-means thinking, why should anyone really be surprised by its effectiveness?

Although many educators refer to "formative assessment" these days, and sometimes rather cavalierly, it is important for you to get an accurate idea of what formative assessment is and what it isn't. Let's, then, consider a formal definition of formative assessment.

FORMATIVE ASSESSMENT DEFINED

In mid-2006, when formative assessment was first beginning to attract the interest of many American educators, considerable confusion existed regarding its precise nature. A number of commercial measurement companies were, at that time, trying to peddle their tests because those tests were supposedly "formative" and, therefore, should be seen as more relevant to teachers' instructional decision making. Although this commercial interest in formative assessment had initially been fostered by research evidence supporting formative assessment, different distributors of so-called formative assessment were using that label in a fairly fast-and-loose fashion to describe very different types of educational tests. Given what was clearly widespread confusion about the actual nature of formative assessment, it was apparent that educators should strive to reach agreement regarding what they meant when they referred to "formative assessment."

In early 2006, I had signed a contract to write an introductory book about formative assessment. Accordingly, it seemed only appropriate that I should take a shot at trying to define what was going to be treated in the book. After soliciting definitional advice from leading authorities on formative assessment in the United States and abroad and attending a meeting in Austin, Texas, of educational officials from twenty-five states about formative assessment, I arrived at what I regarded—and still do—as a reasonable definition of formative assessment. Although modifications of this definition can certainly be offered by other writers, you will find that the following definition is consonant with the research evidence in support of the formative-assessment process. And, as you will see in the closing segments of this chapter, it is chiefly formative assessment's research support that has triggered today's interest in this assessment-rooted instructional strategy:

> Formative assessment is a planned process in which assessment-elicited evidence of students' status is used by teachers to adjust their ongoing instructional procedures or by students to adjust their current learning tactics. (Popham, 2008, p. 6)

As you can see, formative assessment is a process, not a test. Just as we noted in Chapter 4 that there is no such thing as "a valid test," it is equally true that there is no such thing as "a formative test." Although tests play a prominent role when teachers carry out the formative-assessment process, a given test might serve a formative function in one setting and a *summative* role in another.

> Spur-of-the-moment adjustment decisions by teachers, if those serendipitous decisions work out, should be applauded. But they're not formative assessment.

You may note that rather than referring to "formative assessment," I often employ the following phrase: "the formative-assessment process." This represents, in part, my adoration of hyphens, but also my attempt to disabuse readers from thinking that certain kinds of tests are *themselves* either formative or summative. After all, if a hyphen links "formative" to "assessment," then the resultant hyphenated pair of modifiers, "formative-assessment," simply shrieks out for a wrap-up noun such as "process," "approach," or "strategy." As the above definition tries to make clear, formative assessment isn't a test. Rather, it is a test-based *process* for teachers or students that teachers can use when making adjustment decisions.

In reviewing this definition, note that the process constituting formative assessment is a *planned* one. Thus, although many teachers make spur-of-the-moment adjustments in their teaching based on what they observe going on in class—and such adjustments quite often enhance students' learning—those adjustments do *not* constitute formative assessment. The formative-assessment process requires careful planning regarding what kinds of test-elicited evidence to collect, when to collect such evidence, and what action-options might follow. Spur-of-the-moment adjustment decisions by teachers, if those serendipitous decisions work out, should be applauded. But they're not formative assessment.

As you consider this definition of formative assessment, you'll also see *assessment-elicited evidence* of students' status (evidence of students' current knowledge and skills) playing a pivotal role in the formative-assessment process. The assessments that might be used during formative assessment, however, can certainly include more than most people's notion of traditional paper-and-pencil tests. Indeed, a wide variety of measurement procedures might be called on in an effort to elicit evidence that can lead to valid inferences about students' unseen knowledge and skills. Such evidence-eliciting ploys, for example, might rely on one-item oral performance tests or, perhaps, exit tickets in which students supply responses to a brief quiz as they leave a classroom.

One final feature of this definition warrants our attention, namely, that the evidence garnered from students is used either by *teachers* to adjust their ongoing instructional procedures or by *students* to adjust their current learning tactics (i.e., the techniques students employ when trying to learn). The assessment-based evidence collected may, of course, indicate that no adjustments whatsoever are needed. The teacher might be performing spectacularly well and the students might be learning wonderfully. Formative assessment's test-collected evidence does not *require* either teachers or students to make adjustments. Rather, such evidence provides an opportunity for teachers and students to make an *adjustment decision*.

For teachers, based on thoughtful planning, test-elicited evidence is employed to make decisions about whether to adjust their *ongoing* instructional procedures for the students they are currently teaching. That's right, formative assessment is not used by teachers to make adjustments in next year's class involving a different group of students. Rather, if teachers realize their current students are not making hoped-for progress, then those teachers should make instructional adjustments immediately—perhaps within moments or at least within a day or two.

Many teachers also collect evidence to help them evaluate a lengthy segment of instruction so that, if necessary, when this same segment is taught next year with different students, needed improvements can be made. Such year-to-year improvements based on evaluations of a teacher's completed instruction are commendable. Those improvements typically boost a teacher's next-year instructional effectiveness. However, they are not formative assessment.

Similarly, when students are involved in the formative-assessment process, any decisions suggesting students need to make adjustments in their learning tactics should be implemented in short order as soon as practical. If a student's current learning tactics aren't getting the job done, then it is time for a prompt adjustment of how that student is trying to learn what's supposed to be learned.

As the above definition of formative assessment makes clear, this process can take place if it's only being used by teachers—to make adjustment decisions about their instruction—or if it's only being used by students—to make adjustment decisions about their learning tactics. But, of course, it can also be used by *both* teachers and students at the same time. Later in the chapter, we will briefly review some evidence supporting the formative-assessment process. But first, let's take a quick look at how formative assessment actually functions.

FORMATIVE ASSESSMENT IN ACTION

What does the formative-assessment process look like when it is being used? Well, you've already seen that formative assessment can be employed by teachers and/or by students to make adjustment decisions regarding their current activities. What this process translates to, in practice, is that formative assessment must be a *classroom-based* enterprise. Because decisions are being made about a particular group of students, either by the teacher or by those students themselves, then the assessment-elicited evidence about those students' status needs to be collected by classroom assessments that mesh optimally with significant moments during an instructional sequence. Timing, in formative assessment as in many aspects of life, is everything. Although it is not necessary for teachers to generate classroom tests from scratch, as sometimes district-developed or district-purchased assessments can be effectively used in classrooms for formative purposes, most classroom assessments used formatively turn out to be teacher-made tests.

Because the planning and implementation of formative assessment requires a meaningful expenditure of a teacher's energy, the formative-assessment process is almost always focused on students' mastering a truly challenging *target curricular aim* (identified in Figure 8.1 by the heavily shaded rectangle to the right). One example of a target curricular aim would be a student's ability to engage in careful, analytic reading of a newspaper's editorial essays, and then to reach judgments based on "close-reading" regarding the soundness of the opinions presented in such essays. The duration of instructional sequences covered by formative assessment can vary substantially, but in almost all instances formative assessment is focused on longer rather than shorter sequences of instruction. Typically, instructional sequences of at least several weeks, and all the way up to a full semester or even an entire school year, are involved in formative assessment. The organizing structure on which a given formative-assessment sequence is planned is referred to as a *learning progression.*

Figure 8.1 An Illustrative Learning Progression for the Formative-Assessment Process

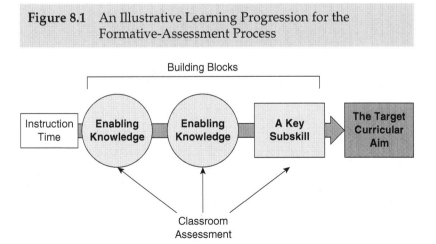

Learning progressions are integral to the formative-assessment process. They consist of a set of sequenced *building blocks* like those in Figure 8.1 where you find a learning progression representing a one-month language-arts instructional unit in a fifth-grade teacher's classroom. In the middle you can see three building blocks. The first two, in circles, consist of bodies of *enabling knowledge*, or information whose nature must be understood (and sometimes even memorized) in order for students to master the learning progression's target curricular aim. The third building block, however, represents an important *subskill* that's also deemed necessary for students to acquire if they're going to master the learning progression's target curricular aim. All of a learning progression's building blocks, then, are regarded as *requisite* precursors to a student's attainment of the learning progression's target curricular aim.

Learning progressions are typically devised by a teacher, but sometimes in collaboration with other teachers. At least a small number of carefully studied learning progressions are now accompanied by empirical evidence attesting to the accuracy with which those learning progressions have been formulated—that is, formulations with appropriate building blocks arrayed in an appropriate sequence. Such research-verified learning progressions, however, are rare.

As you can see from Figure 8.1, toward the end of a teacher's instruction focused on each building block, while there is still some time available for any adjusted instruction to be carried out, classroom assessments are given to students. Such building-block assessments are intended to measure students' mastery of whatever has been addressed in a particular building block (that is, a body of knowledge or a subskill). The evidence collected by such assessments, then, informs decisions by teachers and/or students regarding the need for any adjustments that, if necessary, can be implemented during the instructional time remaining.

Please pause to consider Figure 8.1 for just a moment and you will recognize that it represents three separate applications of ends-means thinking. For each of the building blocks, toward the close of instruction focused on that particular building block, the success of the means being used to achieve building-block mastery is measured by a classroom assessment. Students' performances on these building-block tests, therefore, supply both teacher and students with evidence regarding building-block mastery. If a building block's test reveals students' mastery has already been attained, then it's on to the next step in the learning progression. If, however, the building block's test shows that students are not satisfactorily mastering what's addressed by a building block, then this indicates that an adjustment is needed (by the teacher, by the students, or by both). The proportions of students who must display mastery of each building block are determined by the teacher (for instructional adjustments) and by each student (for learning-tactic adjustments).

It should be noted that one of the toughest challenges facing both teachers and students arises when the assessment data suggest that an adjustment is needed. Teachers typically need help from colleagues or supervisors in figuring out what to do when the teacher's best-bet instructional plans have not gone as well as hoped. Students, too, need assistance in coming up with alternative learning tactics to deal

> Happily, we have empirical evidence that, despite a wide range of settings, this marvelous educational incarnation of ends-means thinking is almost always strikingly successful.

with a situation in which whatever they were doing to learn something seems to have flopped. In brief, both teachers and students need options.

Okay, you've now had a quick look at the way formative assessment usually functions in classrooms. Obviously, many differences in the implementation of the formative-assessment process will be seen because of differences in the educational settings in which it is applied. Some teachers might use formative assessment during only a few month-long instructional units; some teachers might employ it for an entire semester.

Some teachers might rely on learning progressions with only a handful of building-block tests; other teachers might lean on many more building blocks and their related tests. And while some teachers might choose to involve students fully in the formative-assessment process, other teachers might prefer to focus only on improving the effectiveness of their own instructional activities.

Happily, we have empirical evidence that, despite a wide range of settings, this marvelous educational incarnation of ends-means thinking is almost always strikingly successful. Let's close out the chapter with a quick look at such evidence.

PUDDING-PROOF TIME

The ancient adage that "The proof of the pudding is in the eating," as the *Oxford Dictionary of Quotations* asserts, can be traced back to the 14th century. From that distant era up until now, this represents a profound pile of puddings! When it comes to evidence supporting the effectiveness of formative assessment, success-supporting pudding is definitely at hand. As indicated in Chapter 1, credit for bringing our attention to the educational payoffs of the formative-assessment process goes to Paul Black and Dylan Wiliam, two British researchers who brought the attention of educators to formative assessment's virtues near the close of the 20th century (Black & Wiliam, 1998).

In a remarkably influential review of previously conducted classroom-assessment research, these two scholars employed a conception of formative assessment comparable to the one you saw defined earlier in the chapter. Using this notion of formative assessment, Black and Wiliam identified almost 700 research investigations of potential relevance, from which they selected about 250 investigations whose procedures and analyses satisfied the canons of sound research. They then rigorously reviewed those investigations to reach the following conclusion:

The research reported here shows conclusively that formative assessment does improve learning. (Black & Wiliam, 1998, p. 61)

Please note in the foregoing, well-documented assertion, the use of the adverb *conclusively.* Black and Wiliam were not proffering a notion in 1998 that, in their view, was uncertain or debatable. Rather, results of their remarkably careful review makes clear that when formative assessment is employed by teachers, then student learning benefits—*conclusively!*

Moreover, the improvements in students' learning are not trifling ones. As these British researchers continue:

The student gains in learning triggered by formative assessment were "amongst the largest ever reported for educational interventions." (Black & Wiliam, 1998, p. 61)

So, according to Black and Wiliam, they were definitely not reporting tiny, piddling gains in students' learning. Indeed, the levels of learning reported in their 1998 review were "amongst the largest ever reported." (Let's face it, any results reported by British scholars using the term "amongst" are not only immediately acceptable but, indeed, quite compelling.)

And, finally, to drive home the potential effectiveness of classroom formative assessment, Black and Wiliam tell us that their review indicates the formative-assessment process is sufficiently robust so that it can be successfully used by teachers in a variety of ways.

Significant gains can be achieved by many different routes, and initiatives here are not likely to fail through neglect of delicate and subtle features. (Black & Wiliam, 1998, p. 61)

Happily, in the years following the influential 1998 review, other researchers' investigations—as well as reviews by other analysts (e.g., Hattie & Yates, 2014)—confirm the chief conclusions of Black and Wiliam. In the United States, when the *No Child Left Behind Act* was signed into law in 2002—accompanied by its nontrivial pressure to boost students' achievement levels—many educators turned to the formative-assessment process as an attractive strategy for improving their students' test scores. Yet, at the current moment we see far fewer actual uses of the formative-assessment process in our nation's classroom than its proponents had anticipated.

Put in simple terms, formative assessment's ends-means approach to the promotion of students' learning works well by promoting major improvements in students' learning—and there's ample research evidence attesting to this conclusion. Moreover, the formative-assessment process is sufficiently robust so that it can be used in a variety of ways, and yet it still promotes meaningfully improved student growth. Today's most serious concern about formative assessment is that this potent process is not employed widely enough in our nation's schools.

Takeaway Time

Although this chapter's treatment of formative assessment has been relatively brief, especially for such a research-proven instructional approach, for those who wish to learn more about this potent test-based instruction strategy, a number of deeper treatments exist, several of which have been authored by yours truly. See, for example, Heritage (2010), Popham (2008, 2011, 2017), Stiggins and Chappuis (2012), and Wiliam (2011).

Formative Assessment. *The formative-assessment process, a robust, research-ratified use of classroom-assessment evidence permitting teachers to adjust their instruction and/or students to adjust their learning tactics—although remarkably effective—is seriously underutilized.*

A potential action implication flowing from the chapter's terse depiction of the formative-assessment process is for you to exercise whatever influence you have to increase the likelihood that formative assessment will be used more widely. The more that formative assessment is used, the more that students will learn. Those two "mores," then, constitute goals to be seriously sought. If you're a teacher, learn about the basics of formative assessment and take it out for a test drive. If you're a parent of a student, find out if your child's teacher is using formative assessment and, if not, toss a "Why not?" the teacher's way. If you're a policymaker or a school administrator, exercise a bit of gentle (or not so gentle) nudging to get this terrific assessment-based instructional process used.

9

Students' Affect

Underappreciated, Undermeasured

Have you ever watched kindergarten children head off to school? If so, can you remember how flat-out happy they were—just to be going to school? Well I've seen more than my share of kindergartners racing through their school's doors and, in almost every instance, those youngsters' faces displayed unbridled joy. After all, they were "going to school!"

Well, if you could somehow rent a time-travel machine, then flash ahead for a few years as those very same children arrive at school—watching them as they enter the very same school through the very same doors—you'd be struck by substantial changes in many. Oh, of course, some would still be joyful about arriving at school, but far too many of those formerly elated children would display neutral or even negative sentiments when coming to school. How come?

Well, it's almost certain that what you'd be observing was caused by substantial changes in those older students' *affect* regarding school. What had been a collection of decisively positive sentiments toward school when they were kindergartners had become—for many of those older students—much more negative. Numerous reasons, of course, might cause such children to become less positive toward school. One of the most pervasive causes for students' negative reactions toward education, surprisingly, is that educators simply don't pay enough attention to promoting students' positive affect toward school.

THREE COINS IN THE EDUCATIONAL OBJECTIVES FOUNTAIN

Children's positive or negative reactions to education can be accurately characterized as students' *affect* toward school. More than sixty years ago, a University of Chicago professor and his colleagues provided the nation's educators with a three-category classification system for identifying the educational aims then being pursued in the nation's schools. Benjamin Bloom and colleagues' *Taxonomy of Educational Objectives* (Bloom, Engelhart, Furst, Hill, & Krathwohl, 1956) became widely accepted by U.S. educators, and is still employed by many today when describing the kinds of curricular outcomes sought in our schools. The three types of educational objectives identified in Bloom's *Taxonomy* are curricular aims that are dominantly *cognitive, affective,* or *psychomotor.* Not only were each of these three categories described and illustrated in Bloom's classification system, but different lower-to-higher levels within each category were also identified. Bloom and his associates were attempting to provide educators with a categorization system that could better identify the outcomes that educators hoped our students would achieve.

Cognitive instructional objectives refer to the knowledge and intellectual skills that teachers wish their students to acquire. An example of a cognitive educational objective is when an English teacher wants her students to memorize a list of frequently used punctuation rules. (That's knowledge.) Another cognitive objective is when the same teacher wants her students to be able to compose an original persuasive essay. (That's a skill.) As indicated in Chapter 3, cognitive educational objectives, according to Bloom's *Taxonomy*, could range from low-level *knowledge* all the way up to high-level *evaluation*.

Affective instructional objectives refer to students' attitudes, interests, and values. Although certain elements of a child's affect fall outside the school's purview—such as a youngster's religious or political values—many of a child's affective inclinations are of considerable interest to educators. A student's affect represents a *disposition* for that student to behave in a certain way. To illustrate, if a fourth-grade child really likes to read, both fiction and nonfiction, we can predict with reasonable confidence that in the future this positive disposition toward reading will lead to the child's becoming a lifelong, volitional reader.

> Put plainly, by not measuring students' affect, we send a message to our nation's teachers that students' affect is unimportant.

Finally, *psychomotor* instructional objectives refer to small-muscle skills, such as keyboarding, or to large-muscle skills, such as playing volleyball or tennis. Although the in-school promotion of psychomotor curricular aims is typically the responsibility of certain educators such as athletic coaches or music teachers, students' status with regard to psychomotor objectives is rarely, if ever, assessed by any sort of high-stakes educational tests.

What is currently seen in our schools is a pervasive emphasis on promoting students' mastery of challenging *cognitive* curricular aims. After all, students' cognitive knowledge and skills are what's measured by today's high-stakes accountability tests. In stark contrast, assessment of students' *affect* is rarely seen in our schools. Although this instructional preference is understandable—chiefly because of our accountability programs' focus on cognitive outcomes—I regard the absence of assessment attention regarding students' affect to be seriously shortsighted.

Put plainly, by not measuring students' affect, we send a message to our nation's teachers that students' affect is unimportant. Clearly, there is much truth in the axiom that "We measure what we treasure." Consequently, lack of formal measurement of students' affect sends a signal that affective outcomes lack genuine educational significance. Yet, as you can see in Figure 9.1, students' current affective status is a powerful predictor of students' future affective status and, as a consequence, is a predictor of students' future *behavior*.

AFFECT AND ITS IMPORT

Students' affective dispositions, in my view, are often much more important than cognitive capabilities. Let me try, briefly, to support this atypical stance. You don't have to agree with me about the relative importance of affective curricular aims, but please hold off for just a few paragraphs before you arrive at a firm, unalterable opposition to my pro-affect stance.

For openers, let's harken back to our fictitious set of happy kindergartners, many of whom only a few years later became jaded learners—quite unhappy with school. Is it likely that most of the students who acquire such negative dispositions toward school will ever achieve their maximum academic potentials? Hardly.

Figure 9.1   Students' Current Assessed Affect as a Predictor of Students' Future Behavior

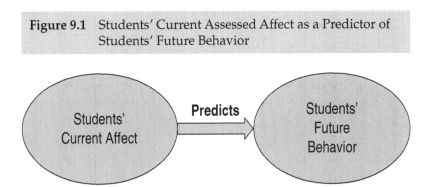

And what about a young student who, even though he is innately gifted in carrying out high-level mathematical thinking, decides to opt out of mathematics coursework altogether because the relentless pressure he's been under (to be the school's "best" math student) has caused him to truly dislike mathematics. He might be able to multiply like a magician and divide like a dervish, yet his negative affect ends up completely extinguishing his positive attitude toward mathematics. Affect almost always trumps cognitive capabilities. Thus, to maximize a child's cognitive potentials in particular content areas, we really need to engender a student's positive affect toward such content.

And think about reading. Surely a child who likes to read as a youth will end up doing more volitional reading as an adult. Educators need to foster positive affect toward reading in order to nurture a future flock of adults who will read on their own. Similarly, faced with today's ever-expanding array of electronic communication procedures, a child who is reluctant to consider innovative versions of technology may be obliged to grapple with today's problems, but using yesterday's electronic tools. Whether students' affect is focused on reading, technology, or just about anything else of consequence, teachers can be especially influential in helping their students acquire productive affective dispositions.

Here's a dilemma. Even if educators do desire or decide to measure students' affect—with the clear intention of promoting appropriate affective outcomes on the part of students—very few of the nation's teachers know how to measure it. In addition, today's teachers rarely possess any familiarity with instructional techniques suitable for the modification of students' affect.

Instructional procedures recommended for the promotion of *cognitive* outcomes, such as supplying students with plenty of "engaged time on task" by giving students ample opportunities to practice what is being sought of them, are dramatically different from the instructional procedures known to be effective in accomplishing *affective* objectives. To illustrate, one of the more effective instructional techniques shown to influence students' attitudes is presenting students with models (modeling)—in person or via video recordings—who will serve as potent representatives of the affective disposition(s) sought. Clearly, many teachers would need at least some level of professional development to enhance their skills in promoting students' mastery of worthwhile affective objectives.

MEASURING STUDENTS' AFFECT

You will recall that when focusing on cognitive objectives, we try to arrive at valid inferences about students' covert knowledge and skills based on those students' overt responses to tests. In the measurement of students' cognitive status, that is, their knowledge and skills, we are asking students to demonstrate their *optimum* performance when being tested. We infer, upon reviewing a students' best-effort test responses, that what we are seeing on the completed test represents the test-taker's optimum performance. But with respect to the measurement of affect, although we still bank on using students' overt responses to engender inferences about students' covert status, the assessment strategy is not so straightforward.

What we are trying to get at when assessing affect such as self-efficacy is also something that's covert, but there's no handy test that can help us determine it. Accordingly, we need to rely on the use of a *self-report inventory* to gauge students' perceptions of their own self-efficacy. In such affective inventories, students are given a modest number of statements or items, then asked to respond *anonymously* to those items.

Yet, even if we ask students to supply *honest* anonymous responses to a self-report instrument, we recognize that certain students will supply what they consider to be "socially desirable" responses. That is, some students completing a self-report inventory will supply responses they think will be regarded positively by those who score the inventory—even though the self-report inventory is completed and submitted anonymously. In short, students completing an anonymous self-report inventory often supply less than honest responses to the inventory because they perceive it as advantageous to "fudge" their responses so those responses appear more appropriate to the teacher or whoever ends up scoring the inventory.

Consider, for example, a teacher who wants to measure his or her students' level of comfort in "being able to disagree in class with the teacher or with other students." Suppose the teacher creates a short eight-item self-report inventory to be completed anonymously, each statement dealing directly with "Comfort in Disagreement." Students are to complete the inventory by making only X-marks on the inventory— supplying no name for sure, and not even any "additional comments" (because the student's handwriting might be recognized). In short, the teacher definitely can't tell which student completed which inventory. However, even though students' responses are truly anonymous, some students will respond to the inventory's items not as they really believe but, rather, in the way they believe their teacher would like them to respond. That is, such "bend with the breeze" students will supply whatever responses they think might make their teacher happy.

> When using anonymous self-report inventories to arrive at inferences about students' affect, the inferences being sought must be focused on the *group*, not on any individual *student.*

On the other side of the ledger, however, because of the complete anonymity associated with certain self-report inventories, some students may do just the opposite. More specifically, because students' responses are anonymous, some of those "now invisible" students might capitalize on this untraceable opportunity to supply false responses to the self-report inventory. Such students might want to "get even" with a teacher for a myriad of possible reasons. In short, with many anonymous self-report inventories, a certain number of students are foreseeably apt to supply more positive "suck-up" responses as well as more negative "stick-it" responses than they truly possess.

And this is why, when teachers attempt to assess students' affect, they must only arrive at *group-based inferences*, not *individual inferences*. Yes, that's right, when using anonymous self-report inventories to arrive at inferences about students' affect, the inferences being sought must be focused on the *group*, not on any individual *student*. When some students respond too positively, and other students respond too negatively, those two conflicting off-target responses tend to cancel each other out—at least to some extent. As a consequence, identifying the *midpoint* in a group of affective responses from a group of students often supplies teachers with a sufficiently accurate fix regarding students' covert affect. By arriving at inferences about an entire group of students, a teacher can still secure valuable information about a student group's affective dispositions—information that can definitely inform the teacher about how to supply upcoming instruction—particularly upcoming instruction related to the promotion of appropriate attitudes, interests, and values of students.

As you can see, then, the results of a teacher's use of anonymously completed self-report affective inventories can guide a teacher's instructional decisions. Affective self-report inventories are of no use in a teacher's dealing with individual students. Not only are such inventories insufficiently accurate in many instances but, let's face it, the darn things are anonymous!

Okay, you've seen that a serviceable way of measuring a student group's affective dispositions is to employ a self-reported inventory to be completed anonymously, and to derive group-focused but not student-focused inferences from students' responses. Let's consider an example of such an inventory to see how these inventories look. Please consider Figure 9.2 and the illustration of a self-report affective inventory intended for students in Grades 4 through 6. You will see it consists of only eight statements and focuses on only two affective perceptions on the part of students. Four of the items deal with students' sense of "safety at school," while four of the items relate to a student's "learning confidence." It is possible to employ only two items per affective variable, or more than the four items per affective variable seen in Figure 9.2. These choices depend on how many statements seem reasonable for deriving a group-focused inference, and how many affective dimensions are of interest to the teacher.

In each set of four items, two are intended to evoke a positive response from a student, and two are intended to secure a negative response. To illustrate, if a student felt very safe while at this particular school, a "True for me" response should be given to Items 3 and 6, while a "Not true for me" response should be given to Items 2 and 8. Similarly, a student possessing great confidence as a learner would supply "True for me" responses to Items 1 and 5, yet "Not true for me" responses to Items 4 and 7.

Figure 9.2 An Illustrative Affective Inventory for
Grade 4 Through 6 Students

SCHOOL: MY SAFETY, MY CONFIDENCE

Directions: Please indicate whether each of the following statements is true for you. Some of the statements are positive, and some are negative. There are no right or wrong answers, so please answer honestly *for you.* Don't write your name on this sheet, only make X-marks.

Here is a sample:	Response		
I like to play video games.	Not true for me.	True for me.	I am not sure.

When you are finished, a student will collect your inventory and place it in a sealed envelope. The completed forms will then be tallied by the three-student committee you chose at the start of the year. Results will be used to make improvements in our class.

Statements	Response (one per statement)		
1. When I am asked to learn something new, I know I can do it.	Not true for me.	True for me.	I am not sure.
2. There are times at school when I just don't feel safe.	Not true for me.	True for me.	I am not sure.
3. The teachers at my school know how to take care of me.	Not true for me.	True for me.	I am not sure.
4. When I must read something new, I'm not sure I can.	Not true for me.	True for me.	I am not sure.
5. I am never given a learning problem that I can't solve.	Not true for me.	True for me.	I am not sure.
6. My family knows for sure that I will be safe at this school.	Not true for me.	True for me.	I am not sure.
7. I often have trouble learning new things I'm asked to learn.	Not true for me.	True for me.	I am not sure.
8. Sometimes, not often, I really get scared at school.	Not true for me.	True for me.	I am not sure.

The statements employed in these sorts of self-report affective inventories can be quite different, as can be students' response schemes. The most frequently used affective self-report inventories are usually modeled after a *Likert Inventory* in which respondents indicate the extent to which they agree or disagree with a series of statements (for instance, "strongly agree," "agree," "uncertain," "disagree," or "strongly disagree"). Some of the statements in a Likert inventory are framed positively and some are framed negatively. Whereas certain Likert inventories focus on only one affective variable for a complete inventory, other Likert inventories attempt to measure several affective dispositions at one time by using varied item foci in a single inventory.

IMPACT ON A TEACHER'S INSTRUCTION

It is neither necessary nor desirable for affective assessments to be forced on teachers in order for assessment-influenced affective instruction to transpire. But if teachers, all by themselves, decide to measure their students with regard to a modest number of significant affective variables such as students' enjoyment of learning—some measurement of affect will, almost certainly, lead to teachers' giving at least a little attention to affect. Moreover, the amount of instructional attention teachers need to devote to affect can be quite minimal. Indeed, on many occasions, teachers will be able to seamlessly supply modest attention during their regular instruction to the promotion of such values as "the importance of a student's *effort* to that student's future success." I believe such increased attention to students' affect would benefit our students.

TAKEAWAY TIME

The title of this chapter foreshadows—and not too subtly—what was addressed in the chapter, namely, our current under-valuing of students' affective status as well as a concomitant dearth of affectively focused assessment devices. Both of those shortcomings are, as suggested in the chapter, readily correctable. If you wish to dig more deeply into affective assessment than was provided in this "once over, lightly" consideration of affective assessment, I've treated the topic in much more detail elsewhere (Popham, 2017). As has been true in what you've been reading about so far, the measurement of students' affect, though not fools' play, simply requires occasional dollops of common sense.

The chapter's treatment of affective assessment boils down to its understanding about the measurement of students' affect:

Affective Assessment. *Because students' in-school affective dispositions can have a significant impact on students' success, both during school and after its conclusion, student affect should be more frequently assessed via anonymously completed self-report inventories.*

Let's head, now, to the book's final chapter where you will find a complete set of the per-chapter understandings that you've encountered thus far—plus a number of actionable responses for you to consider.

10

What Next?

You've arrived, almost, at the end of this book's dash through educational testing's essentials, and its final chapter will consist of four quite separate sandboxes. If you don't care to play in any of them, please employ your page-turning prowess. The chapter revolves around the issue of what a reader of this brief book will do, if anything, with the insights, if any, gained from it.

First off, you'll find the understandings that were identified at the close of each of the book's first nine chapters. Unless you possess really fine recollection powers and have already memorized verbatim those nine understandings, rounding all nine of them up in one place can be useful, if only for purposes of a look-back review. You'll encounter them, a few paragraphs from now, in a section identified as Chapter Chunk 1.

Also, as I promised in the first chapter, you will have an opportunity to retake the confidence inventory that was presented in Chapter 1. It's called Chapter Chunk 2. If you decide to retake the inventory I'd suggest you complete the inventory *before* you review the nine per-chapter understandings, because a recent rereading of those nine assessment understandings might artificially inflate your confidence. After all, unless you are markedly atypical, you won't reread the nine understandings every day, or even every other day.

As I stressed throughout the book, educational testing rests completely on an application of common sense. This is an instance where you can use your own common sense in deciding whether to review the nine understandings before diving into the confidence inventory. Whatever your decision regarding Chapter Chunk 2, the confidence inventory itself is presented on page 125 (and its interpretation key is given on the following page).

The third chapter chunk takes a gander at the sorts of book-based actions that might be undertaken by each of the five target audiences for whom this book was written. Chapter Chunk 3, therefore, spells out a pair of illustrative next steps for those who, having snared the assessment ideas identified in the book, decide they want to "do something" on the basis of such understandings. While conceding that many readers, even if they grasp the nature of the book's assessment understanding, will choose to do nothing about those understandings, this third chapter chunk attempts to nudge readers a bit down an action-taking trail.

Finally, in Chapter Chunk 4, I want to spend a very few paragraphs in supplying three quick, personal takes on what I regard as the most serious issues we currently face regarding educational testing. As I indicated in the preface, a complete career's worth of experience has led me to conclude that educational assessment—*all by itself*—constitutes one of the very most effective ways we have at hand for improving children's learning. I'd like to identify a few things we need to do if we are going to get the most educational mileage out of educational assessments. If we can correct certain shortcomings in the way we currently misuse educational testing, then such testing can catalytically enhance the way we educate students.

And, of course, if you haven't already used the book's glossary, it is patiently resting at the end of the book—as all properly trained glossaries have been directed to do. This book's glossary contains brief definitions of the book's terms identified in an *italicized and boldface* font. Because I personally wrote all of the glossary's definitions myself, I'd consider it a special favor if you'd toss even a tokenistic reading at a few of them.

Chapter Chunk 1: The Per-Chapter Understandings

These understandings are not presented in order of importance, but only according to the order of their per-chapter appearance. To facilitate your review of the book's content associated with any of these understandings, in case you wished to head back in the book to reread what led up to a particular understanding, parenthetical designations have been added signifying the chapter in which each understanding was born.

Nine Assessment-Related Understandings

Twin Motivations for Assessment Knowledge: *Those who care about our schools should understand educational-assessment basics not only because inappropriate tests often lead to mistaken high-stakes decisions but also because classroom formative assessment is being underused.* (Chapter 1)

Purposeful Educational Testing: *The construction and evaluation of educational tests should be profoundly influenced by one of the three primary purposes of such testing, namely, (1) comparisons among test-takers, (2) improvement of ongoing instruction and learning, or (3) evaluation of instruction.* (Chapter 2)

Standardized Test Development. *Although essentially identical to the procedures used when teacher-made classroom tests are built, the development of standardized assessments relies on particularly careful test-building and more complete—yet plain-language explainable—documentation of purpose-determination,* *content selection, and item construction/revision.* (Chapter 3)

Assessment Validation. *Assessment validation, the most significant process in all of educational testing, culminates in the creation of a validity argument based on evidence of both the inference accuracy and the contribution of a test to the accomplishment of the chief purpose for which the test is used.* (Chapter 4)

Assessment Reliability. *Assessment reliability, the consistency with which an educational test measures what it's measuring, is indicated by three conceptually different kinds of evidence and can be calculated either for test-taker groups or for individual test-takers.* (Chapter 5)

Fairness in Testing. *Fairness in educational testing, now seen to be as important as validity and reliability in the construction and evaluation of tests, must be carefully documented—employing both judgmental and empirical procedures—to maximally minimize assessment bias.* (Chapter 6)

Score-Reporting Rudiments. *Because test-based inferences about student groups, or about individual students, are typically formulated from score reports, users of such reports should demand that the scores being reported are both easily interpretable and have been elicited by a test whose purpose coincides with those inferences.* (Chapter 7)

Formative Assessment. *The formative-assessment process, a robust, research-ratified use of classroom-assessment evidence permitting teachers to adjust their instruction and/or students to adjust their learning tactics—although remarkably effective—is seriously underutilized.* (Chapter 8)

Affective Assessment. *Because students' in-school affective dispositions can have a significant impact on students' success, both during school and after its conclusion, student affect should be more frequently assessed via anonymously completed self-report inventories.* (Chapter 9)

CHAPTER CHUNK 2: A REPRISE OF THE CONFIDENCE INVENTORY

As noted above, the confidence inventory provided at the beginning of the book is once more presented here, as is its scoring and interpretation guide on the following page. If you can recall what was described two chapters ago (in Chapter 8), especially the chief features of a self-report *affective* inventory described there, you will surely recognize that this kind of confidence inventory constitutes an attempt to measure a distinctive sort of affective dimension, namely, your own comfort in understanding the topics addressed earlier in this book. To challenge your estimated confidence a bit, the statements in the inventory generally describe activities calling for someone to explain a specific assessment concept or procedure. The inventory's items describe activities about which you are to register your confidence in being able to carry out such an activity. The statements in the inventory address most of the key content in the book itself.

Clearly, the hope is that you will have gained greater confidence regarding many aspects of educational assessment as you read through this book and contemplated its contents. Because one's confidence typically varies from field to field, a person might be super confident about educational testing, yet far less confident, for example, if asked to construct or fly a drone aircraft. What the book's confidence inventory measures, then, is an important affective variable related to the field of educational assessment. If a group of parents, or a group of educators, have completed a short-duration workshop dealing with the basics of educational testing, then you would anticipate a meaningful *group* increase in the workshop attendees' self-reported confidence.

Confidence inventories similar to the one used in this book, incidentally, can often serve as suitable stand-ins when attempting to assess students' skills in carrying out particularly complex tasks such as those requiring the extended participation of several other students. For instance, if the focus of an extended teaching unit is to increase students' interpersonal skills in completing a multiday collaborative *performance task*—but the practical realities of the setting preclude assessing those interpersonal skills in action—the use of anonymous confidence inventories can often provide an indication of whether students believe they have acquired the sought-for skill.

EDUCATIONAL ASSESSMENT

A Confidence Inventory About Educational Assessment

VC = *Very Confident*	**FC** = *Fairly Confident*	**LC** = *A Little Confident*	**NC** = *Not Confident at All*

Directions: This inventory is intended to determine how confident you are with key educational-assessment content. *Anonymously,* please indicate your level of confidence if *you* were asked to carry out each of the ten activities described in the inventory. Circle one of the following responses for each activity.

Suppose *you* were asked to	How confident would *you* be?			
1. describe to a family member what is meant by the label "student affect."	VC	FC	LC	NC
2. explain to a friend what the three chief purposes of educational testing are.	VC	FC	LC	NC
3. help settle an argument between two teachers by clarifying the difference between "validity" and "reliability."	VC	FC	LC	NC
4. make a brief oral presentation during a meeting of parents describing the key concepts of formative assessment.	VC	FC	LC	NC
5. describe to a parent how teachers should evaluate classroom tests intended to support teaching.	VC	FC	LC	NC
6. write a short note to a friend who is a state legislator in another state describing what is meant by "instructional sensitivity."	VC	FC	LC	NC
7. explain to a school's principal why there are different kinds of reliability evidence.	VC	FC	LC	NC
8. describe to a new acquaintance how today's concept of assessment validity differs from yesteryear's notion of assessment validity.	VC	FC	LC	NC
9. identify for a group of everyday citizens why it is the responsibility of those who design score reports to make them readily understandable.	VC	FC	LC	NC
10. explain to a newly elected member of a local school board how today's educational tests should incorporate assessment fairness.	VC	FC	LC	NC

Chapter Chunk 3: Understanding-Triggered Action?

You may recall from Chapter 1 that this book was written for different audiences: classroom teachers, educational administrators, educational policymakers, parents of school-age children, and everyday citizens. Do I think that members of all five of those groups need to understand what was treated in this book? You bet I do.

Surely, at different times and in different circumstances, the book's nine understandings will be of more relevance to members of one of those audiences than to members of the other audiences. A classroom teacher who is trying to figure out what's going on with her students' less-than-wonderful scores on an annual statewide accountability test is apt to be more interested in test-quality than others. And a parent who discovers that his child's teachers are implementing something called "formative assessment" will surely be focused on what's involved in that assessment-supported instructional strategy.

CONFIDENCE INVENTORY INTERPRETATION GUIDE

This self-report confidence inventory is intended to help determine your perceived confidence in understanding a set of assessment-related concepts and procedures by securing your estimated confidence in explaining such content to others. To determine your total score on the inventory, simply assign the following per-item scores: VC = 3 points, FC = 2 points, SC = 1 point, and NC (or no response) = 0 points. Overall, then, the confidence you possess after reading this book can range from a high of 30 points to a low of zero. You may find it illuminating to compare your confidence-inventory score after having read the book to your score on the same inventory prior to reading the book. If your confidence score did not go up, you might want to reread the book, but this time more slowly!

However, the initial question to be considered by readers of this book is whether to do anything at all with the understandings gained. It is perfectly reasonable for someone to simply expand that person's conversance with a process that seems to be increasingly important in the way we run our schools. Taking no post-book action at all is quite acceptable.

On the other hand, many readers will wish to put their newly acquired understandings into action. The potential applications of the book's nine understandings vary widely depending on which of the book's five target audiences is involved and the particulars of the situation in which educational testing is involved. To provide a *non-exhaustive* sample of possible applications of the book's content, a pair of per-audience action options is presented below:

A SAMPLE OF POTENTIAL PER-AUDIENCE ACTION OPTIONS

Classroom Teachers

- When teachers find that the tests they are directed to use are unaccompanied by evidence supporting those tests' purposes, they can register their concerns with appropriate administrators.
- Teachers whose school-site administrators are not nurturing the use of the formative-assessment process can urge those administrators to foster greater use of this potent assessment-based instructional approach in their school.

Educational Administrators

- If a school's or district's administrators learn that their students have scored poorly on a state-administered annual accountability test, thereby suggesting that district instruction is ineffective, those administrators can investigate the quality of evidence supporting the evaluative use of that test, for instance, evidence related to validity, reliability, and fairness.

- School or district administrators can undertake a comprehensive "fit-for-purpose" review of all standardized tests currently being used in an effort to assure themselves that sufficient evidence exists to support each test's use for its intended purpose.

Educational Policymakers

- Members of a district school board where few improvements have been seen for several years in students' performances on a state accountability test can identify whether solid evidence exists supporting the state test's instructional sensitivity so that, if insufficient evidence exists, its evaluative function can be questioned.
- A state legislature can call on assessment specialists in that state's Department of Education to describe the extensiveness and quality of educational tests being used by the state's teachers specifically to enhance the quality of instruction.

Parents of School-Age Children

- Parents of a child in an elementary school where students' performances on high-stakes tests are consistently low can urge the school's principal to initiate a program for parents intended to promote assessment literacy—with the clear intention of having assessment-knowledgeable parents push for more instructionally supportive use of educational testing throughout the school.
- Parents of a child whose schoolwork is less than successful might meet with the child's teachers to learn whether the teacher's classroom tests seem to be playing a sufficient role in fostering students' improved learning.

Everyday Citizens

- Citizens who are conversant with the nine understandings presented in this book will be in an excellent position to discuss with neighbors and acquaintances the virtues of "school quality" reports in the local media based on students' test performances—perhaps by requesting additional information about such test's evaluative quality.
- Because school board sessions are typically open meetings, any citizen can attend in an effort to discern whether the quality of test-garnered evidence about educational quality seems to be sufficiently persuasive—then register distress if it isn't.

Although it is not necessary to undertake any actions similar to those illustrated above, given the vital role that today's educational testing play in our nation's schools, it is understandable if an assessment-knowledgeable individual wishes to do so. The seriousness of the test-related situation in which one finds oneself will typically determine whether one wishes to watch this action from the bleachers or to trot out onto the playing field.

Before leaving the illustrative action options open to readers, there's a "group-on-group" strategy that I'd like you to consider. For example, if the teachers or school administrators in a particular school have made some serious strides in better understanding educational assessment, perhaps those educators might attempt to increase the assessment-related understandings of their students' parents. Parents who better understand the evaluative strengths or shortcomings of many current standardized tests can more accurately decide how much confidence to place in oft-heard media proclamations that higher test scores equal more successful schools. The more knowledgeable about assessment that parents of school-age children are, the more effectively they can work with the educators who try to help those children learn.

Similarly, a group of more knowledgeable parents may want to share their assessment-related insights with citizens in general. That's because perceptions of our schools' effectiveness often translate into voters' positive or negative responses to tax-based requests for greater educational funding. In short, if any one of the five groups at whom this book was aimed decide to do so, educational outreach efforts to another group can have a seriously positive impact.

CHAPTER CHUNK 4: QUICK TAKES ON EDUCATIONAL TESTING

I want to conclude the book with a handful of personal views regarding educational testing. Other than my expression of a few preferences (such as my endorsement of increased affectively focused assessment and instruction), I've attempted to dodge positions of advocacy. But what we've been dealing with in this book is too important for me to remain wholly neutral. I will understand, and harbor no vile feelings, if you choose to dodge the book's remaining paragraphs. Your book, your choice.

But I do feel driven to toss out a few suggestions regarding what ought to be done to make educational testing a stronger contributor to the improved education of our children. I promise to be brief. (However, as you probably already know, promises made by an author during the latter chapters of a book should evoke serious skepticism.) Here, then, are three assessment-related issues that should receive serious attention from everyone who has a major or a minor hand in how we educate the nation's youth.

> I'd certainly like to see at least a few age-appropriate assessment-literacy kernels tossed at our students while they complete their education.

Assessment literacy. Too few folks who should know something about educational testing do not. I'm thinking here chiefly of educators, but other segments of society should not be intimidated by the sorts of commonsense concepts addressed in this book. As I revealed in the book's preface, I was drawn to educational testing because of a mid career realization that educational testing, all by itself, could spur unprecedented improvements in the way we were educating our children. Not only could the more savvy use of classroom tests by teachers promote instructional improvements, but the avoidance of serious mistakes by educational policymakers could also lead to dramatically better schooling across the land.

When advocating substantial expansions in assessment literacy, I am thinking of the level of depth represented by what you found in this book—not much more, not much less. And the audiences I have in mind are not only the five targeted groups identified in Chapter 1. Yes, I realize that this array of folks pretty much covers nearly everyone, but I'd add another group to the list, namely, *students themselves.* After all, the results of educational tests are having a huge impact on children's lives—their academic lives in the short term, and their nonacademic lives when school's over. I'd certainly like to see at least a few age-appropriate assessment-literacy kernels tossed at our students while they complete their education.

But who would underwrite the promotion of expanded measurement moxie—not any more than you found in this book—for the target audiences identified? Well, here's a terrific opportunity for private foundations to get behind a mission that, over the years, will have enormous payoffs for our society. Professional associations, of course, might also get into the act by focusing on enhancing the assessment acumen for their members. For instance, national associations such as those composed of principals, teachers, superintendents, or school board members—solo or in collaboration with other like-purposed groups—could make real impacts on boosting the assessment-related understandings of their membership. And, of course, if the financial resources of eleemosynary (charitable) organizations were coupled with the zeal of suitable professional organizations, the impact could be enormous. (I rarely have an occasion to use the word "eleemosynary," hence was excited to write the last sentence—regardless of what it said.)

Okay, the first point I'm trying to make here is that we desperately need more people to understand the sorts of commonsense notions about educational testing that were treated in this book. But this recommendation is just Subpoint 1 under assessment literacy. There's an important Subpoint 2.

Let's be realistic. Suppose *you* personally did not know a whale of a lot about educational testing before reading the book, but after doing so you had grasped the meaning of all or most of the book's nine understandings. Even assuming that you were fairly comfortable with this information, would you feel you were able to set out on your own and reach a defensible conclusion about the appropriateness of an expensive "diagnostic" test that a school district is thinking of purchasing from a commercial test-development firm? Well, I suspect your answer to such a hypothetical question is probably No. You might understand many of the main points about educational testing, but you'd feel less than relaxed about bringing your rather basic knowledge to such an important decision as buying an expensive diagnostic test.

And here's my second subpoint. What you (and the other would-be purchasers of this "diagnostic" test) need is someone who can supply an exacting review of the evidence supporting the test under consideration—and then convey the conclusions of that review to you and other decision-makers in readily understandable language. Face it—you won't know enough about assessment nuances to pull off such a review on your own, and we simply don't have time to send you back to graduate school for a few years so you can become a legitimate measurement expert.

But *if required to do so,* many of today's current testing experts can carry out a stringent appraisal of any test's quality, and can do so in light of the purpose that the test is supposed to accomplish. Thereafter, *if required to do so,* many current members of the educational measurement community can then describe their findings in ways that can be understood by individuals who understand educational testing's fundamentals (as you now do). Measurement specialists rarely need supply comprehensible explanations to others today because, ordinarily, they are interacting with other measurement specialists. What we need, and what we need *immediately,* is a cadre of assessment consultants who are adept at talking about educational testing's central notions in ways that others can comprehend.

To reiterate this first concern, I think we first need to promote increased understandings for many audiences about the basics of educational assessment. At the same time, we need to establish a collection of assessment consultants who can evaluate educational tests and the ways in which they are used, then present their findings in a clearly comprehensible manner. Let's look, now, at a second concern.

The evaluative use of instructionally insensitive tests. A mistake that's currently being made throughout the United States and at all levels of education is particularly galling to me. It is our reliance for evaluative purposes on *instructionally insensitive* tests. A common instance these days is for a state's schools to be evaluated dominantly on the basis of students' scores on an annual state-approved accountability test. The primary purpose of such tests is, without debate, *evaluative.* And yet, according to the 2014 joint *Standards,* a test must be accompanied by evidence that the inferences based on students' scores are suitable for accomplishing a test's intended purpose—in this instance to evaluate the effectiveness of a state's schools. But for most of today's state-level accountability tests there is no evidence— *none at all*—that those tests are instructionally sensitive, that is, are able to distinguish between effectively taught and ineffectively taught students. Without such information, what's most likely being evaluated by a state's accountability tests are students' zip codes rather than the quality of instruction taking place in that state. The evaluative use of tests not demonstrated to be up to an evaluation function is intolerably wrong.

What's almost always happening in such instances is that the accountability tests employed have been built and evaluated according to a *comparative* measurement mission instead of according to an *evaluative* measurement mission. The folks who created the accountability tests, and the policymakers who approved the use of those tests, are allowing an *Army Alpha* comparative conception of testing to muck up a perfectly appropriate function of educational testing, that is, to help determine the educational success of our schools.

> Those who lose out—as a consequence of today's mistaken evaluative assessments—are the students we're supposed to be educating.

We need to bring to the attention of those who choose any high-stakes evaluative tests the stark reality that they may be using the wrong tests. Use of the wrong tests, of course, makes it likely that incorrect decisions will be made about our schools' effectiveness. Those who lose out—as a consequence of today's mistaken evaluative assessments—are the students we're supposed to be educating.

Unused magic: formative assessment languishes. Given that one of this book's reasons for people to learn more about educational assessment is the underutilization of the formative-assessment process, it should come as no surprise to encounter a final formative-assessment rant before the book concludes.

Formative assessment is such a potent way to teach kids more successfully. As a consequence, we most definitely need to do everything that we can to encourage our teachers to give it a try. Surely, as is true with most educational initiatives, it is possible to make formative assessment such an energy-demanding process that few teachers will, over time, stick with it. Busy teachers, as we all know, have limits on their hours and energy. But when used judiciously or, if you prefer, in moderation, formative assessment encourages teachers to focus their instructional attention on clearly explicated curricular targets, design instructional sequences that seem most likely to help kids master those curricular targets, and then collect key ongoing assessment-elicited evidence to inform adjustment decisions.

When students are, themselves, encouraged to take part in the formative-assessment process by making periodic adjustment decisions about their own learning tactics, the learning yields from formative assessment are astonishing. Students tend to become self-monitoring learners. As always, ends-means thinking wins the day.

Although we need to employ a range of procedures intended to promote teachers' use of the formative-assessment process, we must also provide ways whereby teachers can snare the dividends of formative assessment, and yet maintain a semblance of sanity. Moderate use of formative assessment for the entirety of a teacher's career beats—by miles—frantic formative assessment for a year or two, then its abandonment.

To conclude the book, you'll next find a glistening glossary eagerly awaiting your perusal. And then you'll find bibliographic citations for the handful of sources used in the book. It's been nice chatting with you.

Glossary

accessibility The extent to which students are easily able to display their optimal performance regarding whatever is being assessed via a test, for instance, a student's possession of a cognitive skill or mastery of a body of knowledge.

accommodation Adjustments made to a test or the test-taking process that increase a test-taker's accessibility while not fundamentally changing the nature of what is being tested. Students' accommodated scores on a test should be so comparable to unaccommodated scores that they can be aggregated together.

accountability tests Those assessment devices, often administered annually under a state's auspices, that are employed to help monitor the effectiveness of local educational programs.

achievement tests Educational tests, often standardized, whose chief function is to measure a student's mastery of the knowledge and intellectual skills taught during school. "Achievement" tests are often contrasted with "aptitude"

tests that focus more directly on estimating a test-taker's future performance.

affect/affective A descriptor applied to noncognitive outcomes sometimes promoted in our schools—such as students' attitudes, interests, or values.

alternate-form reliability evidence Reliability evidence indicative of the degree to which two alleged versions of the same test are functioning similarly.

aptitude tests An assessment instrument intended to measure a student's performance so that the student's current score will provide an accurate estimate of that student's performance on a future, frequently academic, criterion. In contrast to "achievement" tests that measure a student's current knowledge and skills, "aptitude" tests attempt to predict a student's future performance.

assessment bias This label indicates whether an educational test offends or unfairly penalizes a test-taker because of such personal characteristics as the test-taker's race, gender, ethnicity, or level of familial affluence.

bias review The judgmental scrutiny of a set of test items, often carried out on under development, not yet operational items, in an attempt to identify any items that might be biased against particular groups of test-takers based on such personal characteristics as their race, gender, or socioeconomic status. Bias reviews are typically carried out by committees of educators or other adults drawn from the test-taker groups apt to be affected adversely by assessment bias.

building blocks These are the sub-skills or bodies of enabling knowledge it is assumed students must master as part of a learning progression aimed at getting students to master a target curricular aim sought during a sometimes extended instructional sequence. Learning progressions and the building blocks that constitute them are encountered most frequently during implementations of the formative-assessment process.

cognitive An adjective applicable to students' intellectual activities like becoming skilled in writing a persuasive essay. In education, cognitive variables are often contrasted with affective variables and psychomotor variables.

computer-adaptive testing A sophisticated form of computer-abetted educational testing in which a student's performance in responding to earlier test items determined the difficulty of the items presented subsequently. Because such adjustments in the difficulty of items can better match item demands with a test-taker's ability, computer-adaptive testing typically saves substantial testing time.

computer-based testing When educational tests are delivered by computers, and when students' responses are recorded by computers, this procedure is referred to as computer-based testing. Unlike computer-adaptive testing in which the items presented to an individual student hinge on the student's success with earlier items, computer-based testing refers only to test-delivery and test-takers' responses.

construct-irrelevant variance Variations in students' scores attributable to extraneous factors that distort the meaning of such scores and, as a consequence, diminish the validity of score-based inferences.

content standard A synonymous term that, along with "goal," "objective," or "learning outcome," describe the curricular aim sought for students as a consequence of instruction. When initially introduced into the educational lexicon, "content" standards were contrasted with "achievement" standards—with content standards more descriptive of curricular targets, and achievement standards more focused on the desired level of a student's performance.

correlation coefficient A widely used statistical procedure indicating the strength and direction of a relationship between two variables, for instance, between a group of students' scores on two different tests. Correlation coefficients can range from a +1.0 to a −1.0 with coefficients near zero indicating little or no relationship between the two variables involved in the computation.

cut-scores This is a score, typically a single numerical score such as "number correct," that is used to separate groups of test-takers into two or more qualitatively different categories, such as "basic" and "advanced." The determination of a defensible cut-score on any type of important educational test typically involves reliance on a standard-setting panel that provides recommendations to those individuals officially charged with actually setting cut-scores.

decision-consistency estimates A way of representing a test's reliability, this indicator focuses on the proportion of test-based decisions that are identical. This consistency index is based on the percentages of test-takers about whom the same decisions—both positive and negative—are based on two administrations of the same test, or on two administrations of allegedly equivalent test forms.

depth of knowledge The degree of cognitive demand required of students when responding to a test item or when asked to master a specific curricular aim. Lower-level depth of knowledge (DOK) requirements might demand mere

memorization, but higher DOK items or curricular aims might oblige students to employ synthesis or evaluation.

diagnostic test A test whose typical function is to help isolate a given student's strengths or weaknesses for use in subsequent instruction-related decisions by teachers or by students themselves. When a diagnostic test is focused by teachers on groups of students, such as a classful of history students, a teacher is usually seeking guidance with regard to potentially useful adjustments in ongoing instruction.

differential item functioning A bias detection statistical analysis intended to identify test items that, when used with large groups, display differential item functioning (DIF) whereby an item elicits a decisively disparate response from different groups of test-takers.

enabling knowledge A body of knowledge, such as a memorized list of terms or a collection of important guidelines, that is believed necessary for students to enable their mastery of a more significant curricular aim. Enabling knowledge is usually contrasted with cognitive subskills, also regarded as precursive to a student's mastery of a particular curricular aim.

formative assessment A planned process in which assessment-elicited evidence of students' status is used by teachers to adjust their ongoing instructional procedures or by students to adjust their current learning tactics.

goal An intended curricular outcome like a student's development of a cognitive mathematical skill, such as being able to solve specified categories of equation-based problems. Popularly employed by educators during the mid-twentieth century to describe an intended learning outcome for students, a goal was generally thought of as more broad than an "objective"; also a statement of a curricular intention.

grain-size The breadth of the educational entity being considered, ranging from very specific to very broad. Thus, for example, a small number of broad grain-size curricular aims might embrace the intended student learnings for a particular course, but with curricular aims fashioned at small grain-size, a very large number of such aims would be required. Grain-sizes are also of substantial concern to those reporting students' test results.

high-stakes tests Educational tests whose results are used to make important decisions either about the test takers themselves or about the educators who prepared those test takers for such tests.

inference The test-based conclusion drawn about a student's unseen knowledge and/or skills. Such inferences, also described as "interpretations," are then used for making educational decisions.

instructional sensitivity The extent to which a given educational test is capable of distinguishing between well-taught and poorly taught students. Especially important when a test is to be used evaluatively, a test's instructional sensitivity can be determined via judgmental evidence, empirical evidence, or both of these.

instructional target The curricular aim, that is, goal or objective, to be promoted by a sequence of instructional activities.

internal consistency evidence This is a type of reliability evidence focused on the degree to which a test's items appear to be measuring the same construct. Because many of this nation's early educational tests were developed to measure test-takers' mastery of a single construct, for instance, a student's "quantitative competence," considerable effort was devoted to having a test's items consistently measuring the same thing.

interpretation Synonymous with a test-based "inference," this is a widely used way of signifying—based on a test-taker's overt responses—the nature of that test-taker's unseen knowledge and skills.

learning outcome A descriptor for what is being sought of students as a consequence of instruction. This is one of many synonymous labels for what it is that educators wish their students to learn.

learning progression A planned sequence of instruction, often for an extended period of time, in which a manageable number of (1) bodies of enabling knowledge and/or (2) subskills have been identified and placed in an optimal instructional order for promoting students' mastery of a more ultimate target curricular outcome. Near the close of each of these "building blocks," students are assessed to provide evidence needed for next steps.

Likert inventory A self-report device, developed originally by Rensis Likert, intended to gauge people's affective status. An inventory contains a series of statements regarding an affective construct of concern, and then respondents (often anonymously) indicate their degree of agreement or disagreement with each statement.

National Assessment of Educational Progress (NAEP) is a federally funded national testing program, first administered in 1969. This carefully constructed and systematically administered national test periodically supplies national estimates of students' performances at certain grade levels and in both mainline subjects as well as in a few less frequently assessed subject areas. Administered on a matrix sampling basis whereby different students in a carefully chosen student sample receive different sets of items, NAEP provides no per-student scores, only group-based reports.

p-value This is usually regarded as a test item's level of difficulty, and is calculated simply as the proportion of students who answer an item correctly. Thus, high p-values of, say, .92 would be thought to signify an "easy" item. However, the proportion of students answering an item correctly is influenced heavily by the manner in which a test item's content has been taught. Thus, without knowing about the instructional history linked to an item, it is imprudent to use p-values all by themselves to reflect item difficulties.

percentile A test-taker's percentile indicates the percent of test-takers outperformed by a referent group, such as the students in a national norm sample. To illustrate, if all of a large school district's students completed a new test in mathematics, and a particular fifth-grade student's score exceeded the scores of 87 percent of the district's fifth graders, then he would have scored at the 87th percentile on the new math test.

performance-level categories Classifications employed as a way of signifying the quality of a student's performance on a test, for example, when cut-scores are used to place a student in such performance categories as *distinguished, proficient,* or *unacceptable* based on the student's test scores.

performance task The task that a student must perform during a performance test typically calls for the student to complete a sometimes complex, particularly demanding task, such as writing a sophisticated analysis of a complicated real-world science problem.

A continuing deterrent to the use of performance tests has been the costs associated with their scoring—because of the need for human scorers. As electronic technology continues to make reduced-cost scoring procedures affordable, it is expected that we will see the increased use of performance tests.

psychometrician A specialist in the development, refinement, administration, and analysis of results for educational tests.

psychomotor Educational outcomes associated with small-muscle and large-muscle skills, such as might be encountered in an automotive class or a physical education course.

raw score Typically the number of items a student answers correctly on a test, the raw score can sometimes accommodate the compilation of items weighted differently.

reliability Consistency of measurement. See Chapter 6 for its nuances.

rubric A scoring guide employed to help evaluate the quality of students' performances on constructed-response items, such as student-generated original essays or portfolios.

scale scores Because scale scores can be statistically analyzed more readily than students' raw scores, scale scores constitute a set of converted raw scores using an arbitrarily chosen score scale. Scale scores, without some sort of interpretative assistance, may be more analyzable, but they are less readily interpretable than, say, percentiles.

score report Once students' responses to an educational test have been scored and analyzed, those students' performances are displayed to those concerned in the form of a score report. To the extent that such score reports are not readily interpretable, then a key link in the educational testing cycle typically renders the entire cycle dysfunctional.

score-spread For tests whose chief purpose is to compare test-takers' performances, the more variation that exists in students' scores, the better. Fine-grained comparisons are more likely to carry out when a set of students' scores display sufficiently large "standard deviations" or "variances," both statistical indicators of the degree to which a test's scores are dispersed. The more score-spread, the more accurately comparisons among test-takers can be made.

self-report inventory Of particular use when assessing students' affective dispositions, such inventories ask respondents to reply to a series of statements or similar stimuli by supplying their anonymous reactions to whatever is contained in one of these self-report inventories.

standard deviation A commonly used index of the degree to which a distribution of test scores is widely dispersed. The larger the standard deviation, the more score- spread that will exist in a set of test scores.

standard error of measurement A numerical estimate of the consistency represented by a test-taker's score on two different administrations of the same test or on two different forms of a test. Typically presented as a plus-or-minus potential error interval, a smaller standard error of measurement (SEM) indicates a test is more consistent than a larger SEM.

standard-setting study Nearly always used when establishing the cut-scores for high-stakes educational tests, such studies call for a panel of nonpartisan individuals to review the actual items on a test, then iteratively arrive at a consensus regarding which cut-scores to recommend. In most standard-setting studies, the panel (often consisting of about one or two dozen individuals) is heavily influenced by "impact data" indicating the likely real-world consequences if cut-scores were set at various points.

standardized tests A test that is administered, scored, and interpreted in a standard, predetermined manner. Although most standardized educational tests are developed by educational measurement organizations, standardized tests are also developed by state education agencies or large school districts.

subskill When a curricular aim calls for students to master a particularly challenging cognitive skill, it is often the case that students must first master lesser cognitive skills that contribute to the mastery of the challenging skill. These contributory skills are usually referred to as subskills. In a learning progression, such subskills are regarded as "building blocks."

summative In contrast to "formative" procedures or products focused on the improvement of yet-malleable instructional sequences, "summative" refers to final version, completed procedures or products. Educational tests used in a summative fashion are typically employed to evaluate the quality of a mature instructional program.

target curricular aim A significant educational outcome sought for students, usually after an instructional period of some duration. When a learning progression is employed as the organizing framework for implementing the formative-assessment process, the overriding, final learning outcome sought can be described as the learning progression's target curricular aim.

test-retest evidence of reliability The degree to which test-takers' scores are similar on two time-separated administrations of the same test. Such evidence is also referred to as "stability" evidence of reliability.

universal design A strategy for developing educational assessments that, from the earliest moments of the test-development process, strives to maximize the accessibility of a test for all of its intended users.

validity The degree to which evidence supports the accuracy of score-based interpretations (inferences) about students related to the purpose for which an educational test is being used.

validity argument A justification regarding the degree to which accumulated evidence and theory support the accuracy of intended inferences in relation to the specific purpose for which an educational test is being used.

References

American Educational Research Association (AERA). (2014). *Standards for educational and psychological testing.* Washington, DC: Author.

Black, P., & Wiliam, D. (1998). Assessment and classroom learning. *Assessment in Education: Principles, Policy, and Practice, 5*(1), 7–73.

Bloom, B. S., Engelhart, M. D., Furst, E. J., Hill, W. H., & Krathwohl, D. R. (1956). *Taxonomy of educational objectives: Handbook I: Cognitive domain.* New York, NY: David McKay.

Hattie, J., & Yates, G. C. R. (2014). *Visible learning and the science of how we learn.* New York, NY: Routledge.

Heritage, M. (2010). *Formative assessment: Making it happen in the classroom.* Thousand Oaks, CA: Corwin.

Nitko, A. J., & Brookhart, S. M. (2014). *Educational assessment of students* (7th ed.). Upper Saddle River, NJ: Prentice-Hall/Merrill Education.

Popham, W. J. (2008). *Transformative assessment.* Alexandria, VA: ASCD.

Popham, W. J. (2011). *Transformative assessment in action.* Alexandria, VA: ASCD.

Popham, W. J. (2016, April). Standardized tests: Purpose is the point. *Educational Leadership, 73*(7), 44–49.

Popham, W. J. (2017). *Classroom assessment: What teachers need to know* (8th ed.). Boston, MA: Pearson.

Stiggins, R., & Chappuis, J. (2012). *An introduction to student-involved assessment FOR learning* (6th ed.). Boston, MA: Pearson.

Wiliam, D. (2011). *Embedded formative assessment.* Bloomington, IN: Solution Tree.

Index

A SAGE Publishing Company

CORWIN HAS ONE MISSION: to enhance education through intentional professional learning.

We build long-term relationships with our authors, educators, clients, and associations who partner with us to develop and continuously improve the best evidence-based practices that establish and support lifelong learning.

Solutions you want. Experts you trust. Results you need.

AUTHOR CONSULTING

Author Consulting

On-site professional learning with sustainable results! Let us help you design a professional learning plan to meet the unique needs of your school or district. www.corwin.com/pd

INSTITUTES

Institutes

Corwin Institutes provide collaborative learning experiences that equip your team with tools and action plans ready for immediate implementation. www.corwin.com/institutes

ECOURSES

eCourses

Practical, flexible online professional learning designed to let you go at your own pace. www.corwin.com/ecourses

READ2EARN

Read2Earn

Did you know you can earn graduate credit for reading this book? Find out how: www.corwin.com/read2earn

Contact an account manager at (800) 831-6640 or visit **www.corwin.com** for more information.

Made in the USA
Las Vegas, NV
25 May 2023

72516557R10098